Free to Da

with the
Lord of the Dance

Free to Dance

with the
Lord of the Dance

Mary Austin

EPWORTH PRESS

The excerpt from *Charlotte the Caterpiller*
retold by Pat Wynnejones from Mrs Gatty's
'Parables of Nature', Lion 1984, is used by kind
permission of the publishers.

ISBN 0 7162 0478 9

First published 1992
by Epworth Press
1 Central Buildings
Westminster
London SW1H 9NR

Typeset by Intype Ltd, London
and printed in Great Britain by
Mackays of Chatham, Kent

They cut me down
   and I leap up high;
I am the life
   that'll never, never die;
I'll live in you
   if you'll live in me:
I am the Lord
   of the Dance, said he:

Dance, then, wherever you may be;
I am the Lord of the Dance, said he,
And I'll lead you all, wherever you may be,
And I'll lead you all in the dance, said he.

Sydney Carter

Reproduced by kind permission of the
author and Stainer & Bell Ltd.

CONTENTS

PREFACE

I first saw Mark Austin in his mother's arms. I was struck by his mop of tight curly hair and the shy faint smile he offered me. I was the new Minister at the High Street Methodist Church in Maidenhead. Mark was just over two years old and, with his family, he had come to my Welcome meeting.

As I saw Mark regularly in the activities at church, he gradually responded to my greetings. During his illness we became good friends, and on occasions he would share his jelly babies with me. Jokingly I followed a routine and tried to persuade him to let me have one of his favourite black sweets. Mark chuckled away to himself, choosing the colour I could have. He knew what *he* wanted!

Mark and his sisters, Elizabeth and Louise, were growing up in the love and trust of Mary and Derek. Their relationships were very close and proved to be a great strength in adversity, enabling the family to face Mark's suffering experience and deal with it creatively.

To be a Christian is to have a relationship with Jesus, a trusting relationship like a child with Mum and Dad. Mark loved the stories of Jesus, which he had been told at church and at home. He listened to them on his tapes and he understood that God loved and cared for people. Children of Mark's age learn through story; it is their real world. For

Mark to trust that Jesus loved him was normal and natural. He found his own place in the story of Jesus.

Over the period of his illness, Mark's relationship with his parents developed because of his total dependence on them for comfort. In a wonderful way this closeness to his parents deepened his trust in the presence and friendship of God. Mark illustrated for me the words of Jesus, 'See that you don't despise any of these little ones.' The simplicity of this child's faith was an inspiration to the church. I shall always remember seeing Mark, when he was desperately ill, holding his hand out at the communion rail to receive the bread, smiling to himself as I said the words he loved to hear: 'God bless you Mark, Jesus is with you.' And he is.

I believe God cherishes and enjoys the uniqueness of each individual. We are all held in his love for us now and always. The real joy is that he wants us to love him. Mark knew that!

I was privileged to be the minister and friend of Mary, Derek, Elizabeth, Louise and Mark Austin.

July 1991
Peter Hudson,
Methodist Minister,
London Forest Circuit

FOREWORD

Why would any normal person want to read about the death of a child? Of course it's all right for the mother to write about it – it helps to purge her grief, we suppose. But for us to *read* about it. No. That would be morbid – far too depressing. What's the point in upsetting oneself? Surely there's enough sadness in the world, in our lives, on the telly? Let's find something *cheerful* to read about, something to lift our spirits, something to laugh at.

I wonder is that the way most of us feel, even the committed Christians amongst us? Thank God, Good Friday only happens once a year while Easter is for ever. I don't think you should feel badly if my rather crude words echo your sentiments. I only write them because part of *me* feels like that, wants to cut off from the world's pain and watch endless television sit coms or murder mysteries. 'Human kind', said T. S. Eliot, 'cannot bear too much reality.' I myself cannot take too much pain, and at the end of a day I need my escape entertainment as much as any one. And yet, in my work at the hospice, in my day-to-day accompanying of the dying and those that mourn them, I share in a quite different kind of escape – an escape *into* reality rather than away from it.

There is an amazing beauty in the reality of the world of suffering. The lives of those touched by grief have a stripped quality, a purity, a freedom from falsity and trivia and a selflessness that reveals the wonder of what it is to be human. I talked this morning with an elderly man and woman as they prepared for their last days together. Her selflessness, her love for him and her concern for me are like a light, like a beacon on a dark night. They are part of the light of God, the fire of love at which one warms one's hands on a cold night. And yet, these are very ordinary people. They are not saints, I am not even sure that they are believers. But they are holy, if holiness is about the transcending of human desires to give oneself to another. They have become icons of the unseen God.

This is my world. I live in it, work in it, complain in it, weep in it. Most of the time, it's a job, a wonderful job, but still a job. I go to work in the morning muttering the while and I come back late at night and fling myself on the sofa and switch on the TV. But I have seen and understood the truth of things enough to know that my world is holy ground and I must journey through it barefoot.

Mary Austin's description of her son Mark's illness and death is a description of this world of the dying, of the stage on which the props are cleared away and the extraordinary beauty of the ordinary is revealed under the spotlights. Mark Austin was an ordinary little boy when he was found to have a brain tumour. Mary, his mother, was an ordinary mother when her world suddenly fell apart. Her gentle, quite unpretentious account of Mark's illness and her accompanying of him during those difficult months makes painful reading. Of course it's painful. Little boys are meant to climb trees and pull their sisters' pigtails, not get paralysed and drift into coma and die. And yet, through the very ordinariness of Mary's story we see the real growth of this little boy, his growth towards new life, towards the time when he will be free to dance with the Lord of the Dance.

Mary Austin is a woman of deep faith but she was always

careful not to load her religion on to her son. Perhaps it was precisely *because* of this that Mark, although only five was able to make his own decision for Jesus and reached out to him in a way that filled those around him with wonder. Mary's is a story of life, of a life lived to the full with birthday parties at McDonald's, endless games and fun and above all of friendship with people of every age. There is his friendship with Peter, the family minister, with David the young doctor from the hospital, with Edward, his school friend, and with Peter Teddy the neurosurgeon who saw in him his own little boy. But more than anything, this is the story of Mark and his family, of Derek his father, of Elizabeth and Louise his older sisters and of Mary his mother, his constant companion throughout a long illness. So, although this is a story of illness and death it is much more a story of life; in particular it is a story of motherhood, of the powerful bonds between a woman and her child.

Above all, however, this is a story of faith: of the faith in God which transformed a young mother into a woman of towering strength, able to walk hand in hand with her dying child towards the unknown. Mary and Mark reminded me, as my own patients do, of the Preface of Martyrs:

> His death reveals your power
> Shining through our human weakness.
> You choose the weak and make them strong
> in bearing witness to you . . .

Mark and Mary Austin have been strong in bearing witness to the love of the unseen God and I am grateful to them for that.

August 1991
Sheila Cassidy
Plymouth

1

Beginning

'I want you to take him to Oxford for a brain scan.' Words to chill the hearts of any parents but Derek and I knew it must be something serious that had made Mark so ill in such a few weeks.

A month before, the school our daughters, Elizabeth, then aged ten and Louise, eight, attended had its annual 'fun day' and our whole family had had a lovely day. Derek and I as members of the PTA committee were busy helping. We hardly saw Mark. He occasionally appeared at the refreshment stall for a drink, icecream or something to eat, ran seventy-five metres in the sports and spent much of his time having rides on the miniature railway. He'd had a great day and seemed free at last of the cough he'd had for the last few weeks, bubbling with the energy and health of a typical five year old boy.

On Monday morning he went off to nursery school; only a couple of weeks to go and he'd be leaving, starting 'big school' next term. But just before twelve o'clock the phone rang and the nightmare began. Could I come and fetch Mark early as he wasn't well. He was fast asleep in a chair breathing very rapidly and noisily. He'd been quite well and then suddenly seemed to flop and had gone to sleep. Later he was sick a couple of times so I rang the doctor and passed an anxious afternoon. Some sixth sense told me Mark was very ill. Instead of making the most of a sleeping child and getting some chores done I sat with him. He was very sleepy, his breathing very shallow and rapid and he was running a high temperature.

Our GP confirmed my fears that Mark was suffering from pneumonia and sent us straight to hospital. The shock made me cry – none of my children had ever been sick enough to be sent to hospital – but at the same time I was relieved to be taken seriously.

At the hospital Mark was so poorly he seemed largely unaware of all the urgent tests and treatment he immediately received. How wrong we were. Suddenly, with difficulty because of his breathing, he asked: 'Mummy, why did you cry at the doctor's?' Later when the physiotherapist came to thump his back to move the congestion he amused everyone by attempting to put his hand over his mouth as he coughed!

I settled down to a sleepless night on a chair bed beside Mark. I was up and down several times to him during the night and then suddenly about five o'clock Mark was peering over the side of the bed calling 'Mummy', tickled pink with having me sleeping so close. The doctors were amazed at his recovery. He went from strength to strength that day, the drip came out, and he was given his antibiotics orally. By the time Peter Hudson our minister came to see him that evening Mark was bouncing all over the bed and two days later we went home. Mark still got tired easily and had a sleep during the day, but he was well on the mend, the crisis was over, we were weak with relief.

The following Thursday he returned to nursery school for the last two days of term in order to leave in style! He'd now finished all the antibiotics but on the first afternoon of the holidays Mark seemed extra tired and in the evening he was sick. Each day he seemed a little more poorly. His speech was becoming markedly slurred, he was staggering and falling over, sleeping a lot and being sick. At his routine hospital check up he was X-rayed and the lung was found to be not quite clear. The consultant looked in briefly and told me to take him home and treat him like an invalid. I didn't seem to be able to get over to them that he had been better, was now becoming more ill again, and his symptoms were different. For a short while my worries were eased, but as the days went on I felt things couldn't be right. He was eating poorly, vomiting several times each morning and losing weight. His speech was indistinct and difficult to understand, he couldn't walk far and was sleepy. Each afternoon he seemed to perk up for a little while. Despite how ill he was he was so good and uncomplaining, never failing to warn me in time to help him to the 'loo' to be sick. I took him back to our GP, who arranged an urgent appointment with the consultant paediatrician.

She examined Mark and then pronounced those frightening words. I went home at the same time numb with fear but relieved that I was being taken seriously and something was at last being done. I began to make arrangements for going into hospital with Mark, and the dogs were packed off to kennels. I had already arranged for the girls to go to my sister Carol for a few days and she had come from her home in Bury St Edmunds that day to take them back with her. As they left, for the first time in years my sister hugged me. We were all consumed with worry.

One of the first lessons I was to learn from the experience of Mark's illness was the value of touch. Not brought up to be overly affectionate, I rarely greeted my friends or family, other than Derek and the children, with a hug or a kiss. But during Mark's illness I came to learn the comfort that can be expressed in a caring touch. Whenever there is a touch of care there is an exchange of energy. Through a touch the giver can say more than a thousand words when they cannot think of even one. It says 'I want to experience this with you, I want to try to feel what it is to be in your situation.' A touch can express sympathy, empathy, love, care, compassion. The recipient feels loved, cared for, no longer alone in their anguish. All through the life of Jesus we see him touching and being touched. Always the touch of care and always with a result, an exchange of power. He was not afraid to touch the unclean, he healed them. He healed by touch, the blind man's eyes, the dumb man's lips, he demonstrated his love by washing his disciples' feet. Jesus also experienced and encouraged the touch of others. When the woman with a haemorrhage touched his cloak he felt power go out of him as she was healed. He allowed himself to be anointed with oil. A squeeze on the arm, a hug, even a kiss for someone who is hurting, is the touch of Christ himself. How I came to appreciate that touch in the months ahead.

Mark wanted to go to McDonald's but fell asleep, only waking long after they were closed. I promised we would go tomorrow if he was a good boy. It turned out to be a long time before he finally had that McDonald's meal! I didn't sleep much that night. Derek and I were both acutely worried. I don't think I even prayed.

We had an early appointment and Mark was super. He did exactly as he was told and the scan was done without any problems. The computed tomography scan or CAT Scan for short took a series of pictures of slices through Mark's brain. Mark had to lie very still on a table which moved backwards and forwards through the scanner. As X-rays were involved I had to don a lead apron. Then I stood by his side and helped him keep his head still while they took the pictures. They found Mark was suffering from hydrocephalus, a build up in the ventricles of the brain of the cerebro-spinal fluid which normally flows from the brain

4

to the spinal cord. Mark's symptoms were typical. An operation, routine in that hospital, to put in a shunt and drain them, could put it right. The doctors presumed that Mark's pneumonia had caused some infection producing inflammation and swelling in his brain leading to the blockage. They would operate that day and re-scan next week. We were relieved to know the cause of his illness even though it meant an operation. We were shown to the children's ward and were at once absorbed into that friendly community which was to mean so much to us in the weeks and months ahead.

Mark was very drowsy and lay in bed all that day sleeping on and off. However he obviously took in his surroundings, once getting out of bed to investigate something he had seen, and months later talked about the other patients in the ward. Sarah in the next bed was having radiotherapy for an inoperable brain tumour. She had been very ill and was slowly improving. Mark slept and we slipped away for a few minutes to get a drink. A little searching brought us to the League of Friends shop and tea room. What an oasis that place is in a busy hospital! Bright and cheerful with flowers on the tables, it was to become a very important place to us! I became a regular customer for their coffee and scones. I found myself becoming more light-hearted and less anxious. It was as if it was not possible to remain acutely worried the whole time. A little later while Mark still slept we walked the few hundred yards into the city centre. Oxford was alive with tourists and bright with flowers on that sunny, summer day. All that day, of course, while waiting for his anaesthetic Mark was unable to eat or drink.

Afternoon became evening. Still we waited for Mark to go to theatre. I took him in to the playroom and we watched some cartoons on video and eventually it was time to go. I carried him to the anaesthetic room and held him until he was asleep. To cause him the minimum of distress they didn't attempt to put a gown on him or prepare him for the operation until he was asleep.

The time passed quickly and soon it was time to fetch Mark. He was crying in the recovery room so I quickly reassured him everything was all right, I was with him. 'Mummy my tummy hurts' he said in a voice so clear I was thrilled. I nearly fainted with relief that it was all over. Mark had had an area of his head shaved. 'Somebody has finally had some of your curls, Mark' I told him. People, particularly old ladies, had been asking him for some of those lovely curls nearly all his life. He always said no, he was very proud of them, hating them to be combed, always ruffling them up again afterwards. One of Mark's friends had sat and contemplated Mark one lunch time. 'Do you always eat your greens Mark?' she asked. 'No' he replied. 'Why have you got such curly hair then?'

Mark had had quite a serious though routine operation and needed to lie flat for a few days, being gradually raised, but he was responding well. However, as the next day progressed my anxieties started to return. Again Mark didn't seem so well. He was unable to pass urine, and eventually to ease his discomfort they inserted a catheter. As his distress and discomfort had mounted his legs had become rigid a lot of the time and his speech was gradually becoming incomprehensible. He was crying most of the time. During the night the duty house officer was sufficiently concerned to arrange an emergency scan. I was woken and told what was happening. I was very frightened and sat shaking by Mark's bed, but when they came for him, as always once there was something to do I was all right and could cope. The scan was clear. What a relief!

Next morning things were no better. More doctors appeared, at this stage a mass of faces, but we were soon to get to know them well. Mark was not speaking at all and although had been told he could now have a drink was refusing or unable to drink. His teeth were clenched. I sat and talked to him and he answered me with his eyes; up and down for 'yes', side to side for 'no'. The doctors thought he might be having a series of small fits and he was given a drug known as epilim to prevent this. During the afternoon he was given an EEG. Again he had to keep quite still, I sat with him and read Noddy stories. Over the next few days they were the only ones he wanted. The nurses allowed me to lift Mark out of bed and sit with him lying on my lap, which we both enjoyed. They were very attentive, bringing me cups of coffee while I sat there. At this time we were first visited by Mr Peter Teddy, Mark's consultant neurosurgeon. He ruffled Mark's curls and told us that Mark reminded him very much of his own little boy, Alex. We also had our first visitors from Maidenhead, including Peter Hudson. All were alarmed and concerned to see Mark's condition.

Over the weekend he deteriorated further. He was rigid a lot of the time, slept with his eyes open, couldn't speak or swallow and dribbled most of the time. That weekend we first met David, one of the senior house officers. New to the hospital, it was his first weekend on duty and he spent most of it with Mark. I described him at the time as the most compassionate doctor I had ever met. There was such concern and always a word of encouragement, a comforting hand on your arm. He was very supportive during that anxious time. The weekend saw the forging of a bond between David and Mark which made David Mark's favourite doctor whatever nasty procedures David was required to do to him.

First thing on the Monday morning they scanned him again, this time using a contrast dye, injected into a vein, which shows up parts of the brain stem more clearly. This scan had revealed an obstruction in his brain stem that might be an abscess or a tumour. The only way to find out was to operate. It would be dangerous and difficult, probing through the very delicate areas of the brain responsible for controlling breathing and heartbeat. Mark might not survive the operation. I was so glad I had sat and cuddled him during much of the night when he'd been crying. They cancelled the list of operations for that day in order to devote the afternoon to Mark. All too soon we were wheeling Mark to the operating theatre. They injected the anaesthetic, put a mask over his face: 'He's asleep now, you can go.'

We were warned he could easily be in theatre for four hours and would go to the intensive therapy unit afterwards. What an endless afternoon that was! I think I had made up my mind he would not live, perhaps in preparation. We sat in Mark's room, I could not have left the hospital.

Suddenly Mr Teddy appeared, sooner than I expected and for an awful moment I thought Mark must have died. However, he looked grim, explaining that they had discovered a tumour which they could not possibly remove.

The rest of the day passed in a haze. Mark was attached to machines with wires and tubes everywhere, his breathing being done by a respirator. As I spoke to him he opened his eyes and acknowledged us. But the medical staff responded to this by further sedating him.

Mark might so easily have died that day, and strangely I found myself reliving the day he had been born just five short years before, remembering so clearly things I had almost forgotten.

2

An Ordinary Five Years!

I had woken up early on the morning of Wednesday 17 June 1981, aware of the first contractions of labour, knowing now that the waiting was over, my third baby would be born today.

Derek took an unaware Elizabeth to school. She was five and in her second term at school. Louise, who was three at the time, went off to play with a friend, and Derek and I set off for the hospital. The midwives seemed to think I'd come too soon, but Mark quickly astounded them by making a very sudden entry into the world just before ten o'clock. We had a little boy. What a thrill! Somehow having had two girls we had expected 'mark 3' of the same model but we were delighted. Suddenly our family seemed complete, new horizons of family interests were opened up with a boy and girls in the family. He was immediately bought the smallest pair of football boots available! Derek and I had married as soon as I had left London University with my degree in biology and had always looked forward to having a family. After a few difficulties Elizabeth had been born four years later. From the moment she was born we were aware that we would like to have three children and whereas when each of the girls had been born I felt there was more to come, with the arrival of Mark I felt fulfilled.

Derek went home and told Louise she had a baby brother.

Later he collected Elizabeth from school and brought them both to meet Mark for the first time.

He was a model baby. He'd been quite small, so needed to be fed often but slept well between times and I was able to be relaxed and enjoy my third baby.

Six weeks after Mark was born Royal Wedding fever had gripped everyone. Mark's pram was festooned with red, white and blue, and he seemed fascinated by the pictures of Lady Diana!

Mark grew quickly, soon he was sitting up and taking interest. He endeared himself to everyone with his ready smile. In no time he was a toddler running round, full of mischief and fun. He got on well with the girls, particularly Elizabeth, who felt old enough to mother him a little. I was to find out how very different boys are from girls. Mark chose to play with cars and any other toys usually associated with boys. His inclinations certainly seemed more 'built in' than conditioned!

When Mark was nineteen months old we moved. My father had been killed in a road accident seven years before and my mother, suffering from multiple sclerosis, had had enough of coping on her own. We bought her house, the home I had lived in from when I was ten until I got married, and she moved into her new granny annexe 'The Granary' converted from the garage. By this time Mark was learning to talk and one of his first words was 'Oy Oy', the name he gave his little blanket rabbit, his comforter.

In common with all small children he loved to mimic what adults were doing and Mark would often follow me around the lawn with the lawn mower 'cutting' the grass with his toy mower. If any odd jobs needed doing there would be Mark with his tool kit seeing if he could help.

He was always quite little for his age, very active and with a head of tight blond curls, which only darkened when he became ill, brown eyes and lashes too long for a boy. As he grew older he never kept still and was loud and noisy. Gran used to tell him he took after his great grandfather (my father's father), who had tended to shout. She told him how my grandmother used to say 'Keep your voice down, Alec.' This amused Mark and whenever he was too loud Gran would say it to him, then he would laugh and in no time at all be just as noisy again. After he became ill it always seemed to me that the characteristics which had been most Mark were those taken away from him. He used to run up to me if I was talking 'Mummy, stop talking, stop talking' he would shout. It seemed to be a case of 'Stop talking while I'm interrupting!'

He was orderly, though, his toys were usually kept quite tidy. We would walk down the garden and come across a little row of cars neatly parked on the lawn! On one occasion when his room did get in a bit of a state after having friends to play he 'tidied' it by removing everything into the corridor. Yes, his room was tidy!

He was used to staying in the creche on Sundays when I went to church, and when he was two years old started going to Sunday School. He enjoyed Sunday School and used to tell me what the stories had been about. However he wasn't too keen about performing in public and the next Christmas a very reluctant shepherd went on to the stage clutching a toy lamb and sucking his fingers! The church played quite a large part in his life. As well as Sunday School he went to the Toddlers Club. I had been running the club since Elizabeth was one and continued until Mark was nearly five and going to nursery every day. I was, and still am, very involved in other aspects of church life, and Mark was often there with me, 'helping' and enjoying running around with his friends. He was never a clingy child. This was something that developed out of his illness later.

One of his little friends at church was Jenny. For quite a while when they were three or four years old they were very close. One Sunday over dinner, Mark was unusually quiet, then suddenly burst out with, 'Daddy, how do you get married?'

Derek is in business. Now we sell plants and flowers but then we had greengrocery shops as well and Mark enjoyed visiting him in the shop and loved fruit, particularly grapes. 'Apes, apes' he would ask for from a very early age. When he was older he loved to visit Daddy and help at the market stall.

Mark and his friend Edward started nursery school just before they were three. Six weeks apart in age and living so close to each other, they had always been the best of friends. I had first met Celia, Edward's mum, when his older sister Catherine was at nursery school with Elizabeth. At nursery the boys played very hard and worked very little, I believe, but they certainly enjoyed themselves. If Mark was ever away the teachers couldn't help but notice, it was so much quieter!

He loved Thomas the Tank Engine and in common with all his little friends at nursery enjoyed playing with the grotesque figures of He-Man and the Masters of the Universe. They eventually had to ban the toys at nursery. When he was two and three years old we enjoyed two beautiful summers, and my overriding memory of Mark and Edward is of them running around the garden, rarely with anything on!

Being lucky enough to have a summer birthday he always had his party in the garden. He enjoyed his elaborate birthday cakes! Over the years, as well as a football cake (his first birthday coincided with the World Cup), he had had cakes that looked like his Oy Oy, Postman Pat and a space ship. For his fifth birthday he wanted a robot cake. I produced a futuristic sort of figure, liberally decorated with sweets. I was quite pleased with the result, but not Mark. Such was his faith in my culinary expertise he'd expected a Transformer that actually transformed from a car to a robot!

Carol's daughter Katie was born a year after Mark, and Jake came along two years later. Although they live in Suffolk he always enjoyed going to see his cousins and got very excited when they were coming to see us. We often went to spend a few days with them and enjoyed some lovely holidays there, particularly when there were ponies to ride. A fortnight before he was taken ill we went up for Katie's birthday. Mark had a wonderful time climbing on her new climbing frame and had lots of rides on Gremlin, the shetland pony whom he loved. He was very fond of animals, more so than either of the girls, and when he was two and a half years old we bought our first dog, Meggie. The love Mark showed Meggie was certainly reciprocated, but there could have been a degree of 'cupboard love' involved. When Mark didn't like his dinner for any reason the items he didn't like used somehow to end up on the floor for Meggie! Mark would be told off, but Meggie loved it. A few months before Mark was taken ill Meggie had a litter of eight puppies. Mark took a great interest in the proceedings, saw the puppies born and promptly named the one we kept Jessie after Postman Pat's cat!

He was very close to Elizabeth, a fact that was brought home to me a few weeks before he was ill when she went off to Guide camp for the first time. They were only camping locally and in the car on the way Elizabeth casually said 'Will you miss me, Mark?', and was astonished as he flung himself on her in floods of tears. Arriving at camp she told the others her brother was crying. He was cross and embarrassed but cried all the way home because he missed her. He couldn't wait for Sunday evening when we went to meet her.

I am sure he benefited from having Gran so close. We all experienced the advantages of the wider family. Gran was a wonderful confidante when Mummy was cross or he couldn't get his own way. From my mother's point of view, she saw him growing up as a grandparent seldom does and recalls how as he grew she was able to see first a few curls and then gradually more of him bobbing up and down behind the wall as he ran (he never walked anywhere) along the veranda and in at her door. She also remembers the gabbled 'See you later alligator' as he rushed out of the door on the way home. Gran was also a good source of Mars Bars!

In his short life Mark had just a little experience of the death of others. His godmother had two elderly aunts living with her and he was sad when they died. But I am grateful for the opportunities this gave for us to talk about them now being with Jesus, whom they had both loved. We were able to build on this when preparing Mark for his own death.

A very ordinary five years for a very normal little boy, active, noisy, very much alive. Then that gloomy diagnosis and our happy world was suddenly turned upside down. Mark didn't die that day as I feared, nor in the next few crucial days, as he may well have done. He lived for fourteen more months. Months of ups and downs, of improvement and deterioration, of loving, sadness, hope, laughter and tears. Months in which we all learned so much in caring for Mark and during which our faith in the love of Jesus, and the power of his spirit to sustain us grew in leaps and bounds. He gave us the strength to cope, carried and still carries us through all the difficult times. From the safety of a healthy family I had always maintained the worst thing to face must be the death of your child. Then, there we were in that situation and we coped. I believe that the fear of any situation can be actually worse than the reality. Not to say that the pain hasn't been almost unbearable at times but God gives us the strength when we need it, not before and not after but when our need is greatest. And it is from these times of greatest need that we rise again, stronger to face life's challenges having shared in the suffering of Christ.

3

Radiotherapy

On that Monday evening in the Radcliffe Infirmary I felt far
from that assurance of God's love. I was relieved Mark had
survived the operation but dazed and shocked by the
diagnosis. I could face no visitors, only Derek and Carol.
My whole attention was on Mark, I could not cope with
making conversation. I had not yet learned to share my
problems. On hearing the news, Peter's first thought was
to be with us. I was oblivious at the time of the hurt I must
have caused people who cared deeply and only wanted to
help. At the same time the presence of God in that awful
situation was filtering through to me. The West Indian
cleaner mopped round Mark's room muttering 'Trust in
God, Trust in God'. Carol, visiting in the evening after
Derek had left to go home, cried with me and said 'But even
if he dies, you know it's not the end.' I began to pray like
I'd never prayed in my life!

I spent most of the day by Mark's side. On the Tuesday
morning he was taken off the respirator, but he still had an
airway in his mouth and an oxygen mask. We returned to
Noddy stories and talking with eyes.

That day stands out in my mind as one of the worst days.
In the afternoon Dr Adrian Jones, who turned out to be an
old friend from my teenage years, came to see us to explain
about radiotherapy. Mark would have to be taken daily to
the radiotherapy unit at the Churchill hospital as there is no

children's ward there. It might help, it might not. If not they would discontinue. He might not even survive the ambulance journey. Did I have any questions, they asked? 'Only the obvious one', I replied. 'If the tumour does respond to radiotherapy, what are his chances?' 'Of complete recovery', replied Adrian, 'something in the region of fifteen to twenty per cent.' That evening I reached my all-time low.

On Wednesday the ambulance arrived for Mark. We set off, Mark, Derek, I, a nurse and an anaesthetist who attended Mark throughout the journey. Mark was still breathing oxygen so the cylinder went too. An X-ray was taken which appeared on a screen and the scans were compared with it so that the precise area to be treated could be outlined. This area was marked on Mark's head with gentian violet. The planning done, Mark was taken into the treatment room. He lay on his side, with his head resting on a rather uncomfortable polystyrene block. The lights were turned down and a beam of light shone on his head to align the machine to the gentian violet marks outlining the treatment area. They were treating his whole brain stem and would bombard the tumour with gamma rays from each side of his head. Mark did not need to move. After the machine had treated one side it turned through 180 degrees and treated the other side from beneath. Mark was to receive a carefully calculated dose of radiotherapy in thirty-one treatments, each one lasting just under a minute on each side of his head. Whilst being treated he had to be completely alone, but we and the radiographers could watch him through a small window. He had to keep completely still. At this stage he was too ill to do anything else. Unfortunately gamma rays damage hair follicles and cause the hair to fall out or in Mark's case not grow again after it had been shaved for the operation. Because of the radiotherapy it grew back with a very high hair line neatly outlining the treatment area. We also had to be careful with his skin as the area tends to get sore.

We returned to the Radcliffe. Mark had made it. His first treatment was over. Months later he remembered that trip in the ambulance. I thought he must have been remembering subsequent ones, but he referred to the oxygen cylinder and it was the only time we took oxygen with us.

Mark was still not being fed, other than through a drip; naso-gastric feeding started the next day. However, he was looking better. I soon realized that this was the effect of the massive doses of steroids he was receiving to counteract any swelling in his brain as a result of surgery and radio-therapy. His face was beginning to fill out as a result.

The next day we went for the second treatment. When we got back the nurse said to Mark 'You can take that thing (the airway) out of your mouth now.' To my amazement and thrill he lifted his right hand and pulled it out. I then marvelled that he hadn't done it before! The doctors were pleased with Mark; he was definitely improving.

The staff on ITU were friendly and caring, plying me with of cups of coffee as I sat with Mark. They were aware, as were the nurses on the children's ward, of a mother's need to care for her child and so I was encouraged to suck out Mark's mouth and give him his drugs into the nasogastric tube, as well as washing him and carrying out normal motherly functions.

All week letters had been arriving as the news spread. These letters were so comforting, most speaking of the prayer which was surrounding us. Gradually we were being lifted out of the pit of depression into which we had sunk on the Monday and Tuesday. I began to feel quite buoyant. I experienced that wonderful feeling of being supported by prayer, and daily we were learning how wide the prayer circle was spreading. I have since heard others describe that same feeling. I began to hope. Why shouldn't Mark be one of the fifteen per cent? He'd already survived surgery, coming off the respirator, the ambulance ride, the treatment, and was showing signs of improvement.

I was by now happy to receive visitors again and was somewhat ashamed of having turned people away earlier in the week. On Friday afternoon they lifted Mark out of bed and on to my lap. I sat and cuddled him and cried. I had thought I would never hold him again.

Mark was now to have four days without treatment as it was August Bank holiday weekend. On Saturday morning he was moved back to the ward. I was able to cope as long as I only concentrated on the present. Thoughts of the past or the future were too much to bear. Derek and the girls stayed at the hospital for the whole weekend, I began to relax and had no more trouble sleeping, it was more like being on holiday. The girls thoroughly enjoyed the hospital atmosphere, helping the nurses with their duties. The nurses brought tea and cream cakes on a tray to the play room while we watched videos. Still Mark couldn't speak, eat or drink. He was able to move his arms but without any precision and couldn't support his head.

On Monday just before the rest of the family left Mark was wanting yet another Noddy story. I was hesitating before getting on and reading it when suddenly he shouted at me indistinctly but definitely, 'Now'. I was so thrilled I could hardly believe it. 'Say it again Mark and I'll read straight away!' He did. It was the beginning of a long haul back to comprehensible speech. I gradually understood more of what he said, one of his first comprehensible questions being 'Can we go to the seaside when I'm better?' That same day Mark ate just a tiny piece of icing from someone's birthday cake which we put in his mouth. We were definitely making progress.

On Wednesday we went again for radiotherapy. Now a little better, Mark wouldn't keep still for treatment, so that session was abandoned. In future Mark would have to be sedated. That day he was very aggressive, a normal stage in the recovery from brain surgery, but knowing that didn't make it any easier. I bore the brunt of his aggression! Whenever I got within reach he would grab me and pinch. I was covered in scratches but the emotional hurt was greater than the physical. I felt cross and guilty but a nurse said I was right to tell him off; however sick children are they still need to know their limits, it gives them a sense of security. The aggression soon passed and he was beginning to drink and take a little jelly to eat. Things were looking much better.

It was about that time that I first met one of the nurses, Sue. It must have been about nine o'clock in the evening and I had settled Mark in for the night when she walked into the room. 'I see you're a Methodist', she said. 'Which church do you go to?'

'High Street church in Maidenhead where we live. Are you a Methodist?' I asked her.

'No, a Baptist' she replied. 'But there's something I must tell you. I never take my work home with me or talk about patients, I consider it unprofessional, but last Wednesday when Mark was on ITU, I hadn't met him and had only seen you and your husband around the ward. I went to my prayer meeting. During the meeting I had a strong urge to pray for Mark and I asked everyone to pray for a little boy seriously ill in intensive care. Then I came to work and looked at Mark's notes, saw you are Methodists and thought to myself, the Lord looks after those who love him!' I don't remember my reply. Presumably I thanked her, I was very touched. It was the beginning of a close friendship and Sue's church at Aylesbury continued to pray for Mark and us for the rest of his life. After he had died we went there for a service and were welcomed like old friends.

Sue's words had a great impact on me. Firstly it was a tremendous witness to God's love. I presumed that Sue was evangelical. I have since learned that she is not and it took tremendous courage for her to come and tell me, so much that she had avoided me for the first two nights of her week of night duty! She has also told me how, at the meeting, she had initially resisted the impulse to pray for Mark and then suddenly found herself doing so.

Secondly, her words stung me. Did I really love God with all my heart and soul? Wasn't I holding something back? It gave me much food for thought and in the realization Jesus began to be very real to me. By now I was sleeping in a room in the nurses' home. Mark's crisis had passed and I felt that after camping out in the ward for a fortnight I needed a base, somewhere to call my own. It was a small, plain, rather dingy little room but it was my home for the next six weeks. Each night as I settled down to sleep I would pray for Mark, for those caring for him and for the strength to carry on. At these times familiar words would come to me: 'Lord Jesus Christ, you have come to us, you are one with us . . .', from Patrick Appleford's hymn; '. . . that we may for ever live in him, and he in us', from the prayer of humble access in the communion service. I was becoming one with Jesus, his spirit within me, it was as if I could feel his arms around me as I lay alone in that bed.

Mark still wasn't eating enough and they threatened to tube feed him again. I had a serious chat with Mark and explained the situation. It was up to him. He ate three pots of jelly straight off! He didn't look back; within two days he was eating fish fingers and chips, well mashed up and being fed to him, and the following Monday he had those long awaited McDonald's chicken nuggets, brought into the hospital as a take away!

Mark was growing stronger everyday. His physical ability and speech were gradually improving. It was like watching the telescoped development of a baby. Soon he was able to support his head, and gradually he became able to sit with support and then without. His arms became stronger and more under control although his left arm continued to be weaker. He was very determined, his naturally stubborn character helping him through every step. We felt it had kept him alive. He wouldn't resort to using a baby feeder cup, so drink times were very messy. He hated any aids at all really, only tolerating a buggy. Five years old is a terrible time to lose your independence when you've not long gained it. To resort to many of the available aids was to return to babyhood. For this reason I was glad that Mark never became incontinent. A nappy would have been the ultimate humiliation.

Once he was able to sit with support we were able to push him around in a buggy major, a large version of the baby buggy, made for disabled children. The day after I had first met Sue I took him for his first walk, down in the lift and out of the front door of the hospital to see the goldfish in the pond. Peter was visiting at the time and he came too.

Whenever we received visitors we would take them either to the canteen or the League of Friends for a drink. Mark's Sunday School teacher came and bought him an ice lolly. He chose a big one and to my surprise ate it all quite quickly. Up to then I hadn't been warned that steroids vastly increase the appetite. Mark became an ever open door. Most days by three o'clock he was asking for his tea. Snacks didn't seem to help, he was always hungry and rapidly put on weight. If anyone had told me that as he came off the steroids the opposite would happen and he would stop eating completely I wouldn't have worried. As it was I tried to restrict his diet a little as my always slim son got fatter and fatter. Adults who have taken steroids in conjunction with radiotherapy have spoken of unbearable hunger. A nurse who had worked on an adult radiotherapy ward told me they used to order two lunches for some of the patients.

Derek was on holiday for a few days and he agreed to stay with Mark one day and enable me to go home for a few hours. It was strange coming home. I was glad to be alone for that first visit because I felt very emotional and tearful. The house seemed strangely small. Everything was very clean and tidy as friends from school had been in the day before 'spring cleaning' for us. I walked through the house and looked out into the back garden. More tears filled my eyes as I noticed 'Mark's bush', the shrub he had planted on his fifth birthday.

Derek had been very apprehensive about being left to care for Mark without me around but I returned to find their time together had been very successful. The day before, Una, the ward school teacher, had introduced herself. So far during Mark's time in hospital it had been summer holidays, but now the new term was beginning. Una had called again while Derek was with Mark and introduced him to a wonderful game called 'Tummyache' which he enjoyed playing and had made him laugh and laugh; another first on Mark's road to recovery. 'Tummyache' became a great favourite of Mark's and Una often played it with him as a reward for working well.

4

Hospital Routine

Now that Mark was eating well, not needing the catheter any more and was making progress the doctors suggested that we could take him home for the day and if all went well stay overnight.

Mark was so excited. I had bought him a watch during my day at home and the nurses told me he kept looking at it all night to see what time it was and how long till Daddy would come. He was awake very early and we whiled away the endless time until Derek arrived. Eventually he came and we settled Mark in the back of the car with his pillow for support.

It was an awful weekend although I am sure Mark had a wonderful time. Away from the secure environment of the hospital the responsibility was overwhelming. Also whereas in hospital Mark appeared to be making great progress and we could see how much he had improved, at home, seeing him in familiar surroundings we realized just how far there was to go, just how much he couldn't do. To see him sitting still instead of running or even charging along the passage, to look into the garden at the swings, climbing frame, slide without Mark clambering all over them. To drive in the car without having to constantly say 'Sit down Mark'. By now we were beginning to get him to his feet and with a great deal of help and support he was able to walk a little. But three weeks of lying in bed had caused Mark's feet to drop a little and the tendons behind his knees and ankles to shorten. Therefore he tended to walk on his toes and it caused him a lot of pain to put his foot flat on the floor and straighten the back of his knee.

We didn't do much. Just passed a quiet weekend at home. I went to the early communion service on Sunday morning, my first opportunity to go to church for weeks. In the afternoon before going back, we went with Celia, Edward and Catherine to McDonald's. The children sat at one table and I drew the buggy with Mark up next to me. I then realized this was wrong and put him with the other children. We were aware of a certain amount of reserve between Mark and Edward and were not quite sure what to do about it. We arranged that Celia would bring Edward to see Mark in hospital.

We returned to Oxford. Mark was miserable and cross to be back, and I felt very low. The weekend had been a tremendous strain and I felt depressed with Mark's condition.

Now Adrian decided to try Mark's treatment without sedation as he was so much better and could be reasoned with or bribed to keep still. I had offered Mark his very own box of Roses chocolates if he managed it. But his radiotherapy that day was not successful. He cried when the radiographers tried to leave him and he was not keeping still enough for treatment. He obviously still needed to be sedated.

The following Wednesday Mark should have started school. However, at nine o'clock instead of waving goodbye to my 'baby' and walking tearfully away across the playground I was sitting with him in the ambulance. He knew he should have been starting school that day, knew Edward would be there and that he would come to see him that evening and tell him all about it. Edward came bringing

Mark's first reading book. For the time being school for Mark would be with Una. Mark and Edward were beginning to be a little more relaxed with each other, but that day was the turning point. 'Show Edward what you can do Mark' I said, and Edward was suitably impressed to see Mark stand and walk a little holding on. At dinner time Edward took Mark's arm and helped him walk to the playroom, with Mark holding the wall on the other side. We all went to the canteen for dinner later on with Edward pushing Mark in the buggy. Another time Edward sat in the buggy and Mark pushed! Walking with his feet flat on the ground was still painful for Mark but the physiotherapy he was having slowly started to improve matters, and of course the best physio was walking itself.

Our days now fell into a routine. Mark would usually be awake when I got up to the ward about seven o'clock. Sometimes he had already had his breakfast. He was usually quite happy. After breakfast Mark had his sleeping medicine as well as his steroids, now being slowly reduced, and epilim. The ambulance would usually arrive by nine o'clock and we would set out for the Churchill. After treatment Mark slept while I drank coffee from a machine and read magazines during the seemingly endless wait for the return ambulance. Back at the Radcliffe I would usually manage to get away from the ward for a short while until Mark had slept off the sedation. We passed the rest of the days playing games, reading stories, going for long walks round Oxford and of course going to school with Una. In the early days he liked me to be in the room, but as he got to know Una better he was happy to be there alone. Una became a wonderful friend to Mark. Amongst many doctors and nurses she was always the same and he got on well with his school work under her guidance.

During those last weeks in Oxford our stay became more

like a holiday. The crisis was over, Mark was getting better and better. We enjoyed the time together, particularly going for walks with frequent stops for drinks and ice creams!

After that first home visit Mark was allowed home every weekend. Derek collected us on Friday afternoons and took us back on Sunday evenings. He then as a rule only visited once during the week when, after Mark was asleep, we took the opportunity to have a meal together.

As Mark improved daily there began to form in my mind questions that would have been pointless to ask when the treatment began and we didn't know if he would even be alive the next day. I requested an appointment with Adrian, which was arranged for one morning after Mark's treatment while he was still asleep. David helped me make a list of all the things we wanted to know. He asked me if the nurses had talked to me about Helen House, the children's hospice in Oxford. I was slightly upset at this as I was not intending to look on the black side at that time. We would cross that bridge when and if we came to it. Adrian agreed with my attitude but suggested that if at all possible we should keep Mark at home. It would be better for him, us and the girls, he said. He told me that if the tumour was to regrow it would be most likely during the second year and then nothing further could be done. If, however, more time had passed there would be a case for further radiotherapy. If Mark remained well for five years we could begin to relax and consider him permanently cured. The steroids could slowly be withdrawn, they were already reduced significantly and before he left hospital were reduced sufficiently to take the edge off his gnawing hunger. The epilim he would need for at least a year to prevent the possibility of convulsions after the assault his brain had received over the previous weeks. Adrian would need to see Mark about once a month after he left hospital and if he remained well the visits could become less frequent. He invited me to telephone him if I was worried at any time.

After the abortive attempt to carry out his radiotherapy without sedation we had continued to sedate him every day until, one morning, Mark said 'I'm not going to have my sleeping medicine today.' I asked him, was he absolutely sure and he would have to stay very still and be all alone for the treatment. He was sure, he'd also remembered the promised box of Roses chocolates. We were all doubtful but decided to try. The radiographers were impressed to see him awake and how much better he was. We went in to the treatment room and I lifted Mark on to the table. The radiographer tied a bandage around Mark and the table to make him feel more secure, putting on his seat belt as she called it, and lined up the machine. We left him with his blanket and a picture of the dogs, listening to a story on his tape recorder. He was fantastic. Occasionally he would move a fraction, but the radiographers watching through the window would stop treatment and go in and adjust him. Soon it was all over and I helped a very proud Mark back into the buggy. He then helped me throw away the 'sleeping medicine' we'd taken in case, with great pride. Back at the Radcliffe we went for a celebratory drink at the League of Friends, coffee for me, Cola for Mark, and bought his box of Roses.

From then on he got better and better at keeping still and by the last treatment was so confident even his blanket could be left behind. Being awake everyday had its bonuses and its setbacks. It was great fun to be allowed to press the buttons and return the machine to normal after treatment, to be able to show off how well he was beginning to walk, and also there were the tropical fish to watch in the waiting room, toys to play with and the stories we read while waiting for the ambulance. But there was a disadvantage. Previously

Mark had slept through the sometimes very long wait. Now he had to experience it for himself. 'When is the ambulance coming Mummy?', was his constant cry! There were further advantages in not being daily sedated. He became more alert in the afternoons and began to enjoy his schoolwork with Una more.

Physically, Mark was progressing well. He was beginning to take a couple of steps between objects without help, walking was no longer painful. He was beginning to push the buggy rather than sit in it and was using his hands well, playing with his toys and writing. Eventually, about six weeks after he had first been admitted to hospital, he walked the entire length of the ward without help. I was behind him and couldn't see his face, but other people watching told me of the triumph written all over it.

The weekends at home had prepared me for being at home with Mark and I began to look forward to the end of his treatment and the time when we could go home for good. Our final week in hospital was drawing to an end. At last Friday came. We went to the Churchill for radiotherapy, after which we had an appointment with Adrian, and Mark showed him what he could do. Adrian said how pleased he was, but admitted to me how worried he'd been about Mark when he first met us. I asked whether it was in order to take Mark away on a holiday at half term in about three weeks time: we wouldn't go far. He suggested we go ahead and book up. He would see Mark in the three weeks before half term but we should be prepared not to want to go. This disturbed me somewhat, but I was learning to appreciate Mark's progress for the moment and to ignore any alarming remarks. We were fully aware that even with the marvellous response Mark had shown to radiotherapy his future was far from sure. But the only way to live was to be positive and hopeful. Perhaps this was our form of the denial often shown in the face of threatening news. I don't know, as at the same time I was still well aware of what could happen.

Mark was now able to walk around the house without help. He walked down the garden and with my heart in my mouth I watched him climb the climbing frame. A week later he called to me 'Look Mummy!' I turned round and he ran on the spot. He was even getting in and out of the car unaided. It seemed he had now recovered every skill and only needed to build up his stamina, weakened by illness and the effect of the steroids on his muscles. Although his dose of steroids was well reduced now, they had the effect of causing muscle wastage particularly in the legs and buttocks. Even his speech was nearly normal although still nasal.

Mark came and clambered into my bed one morning. I hugged him. My own little miracle, the answer to all my prayers. I attributed his recovery to the miracle of modern medicine, the many prayers said for him, and his determined attitude to overcome all difficulties. People asked me how the experience had affected my faith. I knew it had strengthened it beyond all bounds. I also knew this was not because Mark had got better but because of the strength and support I had felt at the very worst times. It was an uplifting experience to be the subject of prayer and to feel the love of Jesus surrounding me. I could look back to the early days of Mark's illness and appreciate the growth in my faith. Another way in which I knew I was different was that I had come face to face with death and it no longer held the fear for me it once had. I had always admired those who care for the terminally ill. I have realized that to cope with another's death you have to come to terms with your own mortality. During Mark's illness I had achieved this.

Home at last we now faced the challenge of trying to get back to normal. I had become very institutionalized and found it hard to get back into the routine of cooking and housekeeping. Friends were still very good to us, with many of them continuing to ferry the girls to and from school and their other activities, and a friend offered to come and do some cleaning for me occasionally. Although Mark needed a lot of attention I found I had endless patience with him and I am quite sure that this patience was the gift of God to our situation. Life would never be quite the same again. Derek and I had always enjoyed collecting things, old paintings, antique pottery, and had spent many happy times browsing round antique shops or fairs or bidding at auctions. Suddenly material possessions seemed so unimportant. Quite independently Derek and I had the feeling that we would like to get rid of all we had collected. We didn't do so because the effort would have been too much, but we no longer gained pleasure searching for new finds, it all seemed so trivial. The last two months had turned our world upside down but it had also given me a growing faith that the love of Jesus would sustain and support me through whatever I might have to face. I bought a poster for the kitchen wall which said everything I felt. An alsatian puppy peering tentatively through a hole in a fence says; 'You won't let anything come my way that we can't handle together.'

5

Home Again

Pleased as I was to be at home, I missed the security and company of the hospital, but Mark and I quickly began to fill our days with all sorts of activity. He was thrilled to be home and well enough to enjoy his toys, to be able to run about again and to talk normally.

We had to return to Oxford the next Thursday for a scan. My hopes that nothing would be seen on the scan were unrealistic but the tumour was shown to be degenerative and as the radiotherapy would still be working they could expect further improvement. There was a cyst on the degenerative tumour tissue but there was no way of knowing if it consisted of live or dead cells. Still, Mark had made an excellent recovery and everyone was very pleased.

Within a couple of weeks he was reasonably independent of physical help, only needing the buggy for long distances, He could even walk down a flight of stairs unaided.

He started to spend an hour three times a week after school time with his teacher and quickly progressed with his school work, looking forward to the time when he could go to school full time with his friends. I asked when this might be because he was so well and his teacher judged him to be well up with the rest of his class. They seemed reluctant to have him initially because of the responsibility. Mark thoroughly enjoyed his private lessons but longed to be there with his friends. Although he enjoyed learning, school to him was also a place to meet with and play with his friends.

Half term and Mark's appointment with Adrian were upon us. When it was our turn Mark showed off all he could do and went off for a short walk and run round the clinic with Adrian' who was delighted. Although he said it was early days he was very hopeful. We could gradually wean him off the steroids over the next three weeks. Mark was pleased at yet another sign that he was getting better. He continued to improve, even learning to swim with arm bands during this time.

But as the steroids were reduced Mark's appetite started getting poorer. Initially I wasn't concerned as he had a lot of weight to lose and we were pleased as his bloated face returned to normal and he became once again the Mark we knew.

But before long we could hardly get him to eat anything. As he refused meal after meal we became anxious, we hadn't been warned of this possible side effect of steroid reduction. When we did tempt him with McDonald's he ate and was promptly sick.

We went swimming; and watching Mark walking round the pool in his swimming trunks I detected a slight stiffness in his left leg but wasn't sure if it was something I hadn't noticed before when he was wearing trousers. We had been beginning to plan Christmas. I had even been daring to think what present to buy for Mark. Now I began to fear he might not still be with us for Christmas.

I was really beginning to worry again.

Finally I could no longer put off ringing the hospital and soon, about six weeks after leaving hospital, we were on our way back to Oxford. Mark lay in the back of the car, very dejected. We wondered what must be going through his mind. He had with him his new water pistol, which he intended to squirt at David!

Mark walked into the hospital with us and we met David at the bottom of the stairs. Mark was pleased to see him and the water pistol was fired! David then took it and Mark got wet too! But there was much laughter and Mark seemed a little happier. In the ward David examined his eyes (the blood vessels in the retina reveal any pressure within the brain) and announced that he thought everything was OK but would arrange a scan just to make sure. The difference in Mark was amazing. We went off to get a drink while we waited for the scan and he ran ahead of us along the corridor. Just the thought of hospital had made him tired and lethargic. The scan supported David's diagnosis. We were most reassured; his symptoms were all to do with steroid reduction. David suggested we finish them altogether as soon as possible in the hope that Mark would soon start to eat properly. About the only thing he was eating happily was sweets and I must confess whereas I had always been very careful about my children's diet I was happy for him to have anything that would give him calories. However, although reassured that the tumour wasn't regrowing, I was aware that the situation was not improving.

When he did eat he started to develop food fads. I have since found out that food fads are also a side effect of steroids, and for the rest of Mark's life his diet was dominated by whatever the current fad was. We went from Yorkshire pudding to McDonald's hamburgers, to toasted bacon sandwiches, cereal bars and even Ferrero Rocher chocolates, to name but a few. At times his diet would consist almost entirely of the current fad.

He started to develop colds and coughs, his walking wasn't so good and he didn't run so much. Again, his steroid dependency lowered his resistance to infection.

Noticing his right eye was turning in and he was appearing to hold his head to one side was the last straw and I phoned Adrian. He attributed all the problems to the finishing of the steroids and suggested I start to give him a small dose again!

The steroids made some improvement and our anxiety eased. The next Sunday was my birthday. I slipped out of the house before anyone was awake and went to the early communion service, delighted to be able to start my birthday in that kind of fellowship with Jesus. I told Mark that the best birthday present he could give me would be to eat up all his dinner, which he did. We went out for lunch to a hotel where a swim is included. We all swam before lunch and then Derek, my mother and I sat and drank our coffee and watched while the children went in again. We were amused to watch Mark swim right across the pool trying to grab hold of a big float he wanted to play with.

A few days later we had an appointment with Adrian. I told him that Mark never ran anymore. We opened the door to leave and he ran into the waiting room. For a split second I was relieved until he fell flat on his face. He never ran again. I began to realize I was pleased whenever I saw him walk just a few steps on his own.

The next morning was a nightmare for me because he coughed all through the pantomime we had gone to see and was plainly not well again. I was becoming really frightened. How could I watch him deteriorate after seeing his pleasure as he had recovered? How could I bear it if he died?

I rang and a doctor came to see Mark. Sure enough he had another chest infection. By now it was early evening and I rushed straight out to the only chemist that was still open. They locked their doors as I left. When I got home, as I got out of the car I dropped the bottle of antibiotics and smashed it on the drive. I was so upset. However a friend from the church who is a pharmacist offered to ring the doctor to check the dose and arrange for another prescription, get another bottle of medicine, and bring it round later in the evening.

Mark was now spending an hour at school some days with a welfare assistant to help him in the classroom. Soon he was to go for one hour every day, and the after-school sessions finished. It is a point of great sadness to me that during those weeks when Mark was best physically and would have gained most out of being at school he wasn't able to go. By the time he did go he was already weaker.

One morning I rang to say he wouldn't be there as he wasn't too well and needed to have all his strength for the Christmas party at the Radcliffe Infirmary that afternoon. We arrived in Oxford in plenty of time. Mark wouldn't go in the buggy and insisted on pushing it instead. We met Una as we walked along the road into the hospital, and soon we were meeting up with children and parents we had met during our stay in hospital. It was a thrill to see so many of them and see them so well.

The first game was musical mat and Mark won it. Unfortunately, because he won he had had to walk round for so long he was tired and didn't want to play anything else. He told me he had kept hoping he would land on the mat and be out as he had had enough of walking and his legs were tired.

I enjoyed the party and felt happier than I had for some time. Seeing Mark amongst other sick children made him seem better and I was reassured. Mark's only disappointment that day was that he didn't see David. What he didn't know was that David, in the guise of Father Christmas, saw him. Father Christmas arrived with a pillow stuffed down the front of his red suit and a sack of presents on his back.

The children gathered round. Mark was fairly near the back but slowly edged his way forward. Father Christmas was saying to each child, 'Hello, how are you?' and giving him or her a present. Eventually it was Mark's turn. 'Hello Mark, how are you?' asked Father Christmas. I cringed. Would Mark notice that David had known his name and wonder how he knew? He didn't say anything and I thought he hadn't noticed until on the way home he suddenly said, 'Father Christmas must have remembered my name from the Toy Fair (a school event where he'd seen Father Christmas a few weeks before) but he's much fatter than he was then!'

When Mark had first left hospital we had been encouraged to apply for a disabled persons parking badge for the car so that we could park on double yellow lines for a limited period. I had applied but been told that the waiting list for assessment was very long and we were not given an appointment until December. At the time, seeing Mark's initial progress, I had felt that by then he would be perfectly normal, but I had still kept the appointment. However by December he couldn't walk far and was awarded the badge. I know there were people who thought I was wrong to apply and this was upsetting, but there was no way Mark could walk all round town and the badge made things so much easier. Even with the buggy, parking in carparks was difficult because it was much bigger than a baby buggy. We could now park in the High Street and Mark could walk into one or two shops or into McDonald's. He hated to use the buggy so much and it helped him maintain his independence just a little bit longer.

6

Christmas '86

Christmas was fast approaching and with it very mixed feelings: great joy and thanksgiving that after the traumas of the past year Mark was indeed with us to celebrate combined with severe anxiety as I saw his condition worsening. There was no peace for me in the festive season that year. But Mark was getting excited; hospital party, school events, writing cards and choosing presents were all part of the preparation for him. Also an important part of the season were the stories of Jesus being born as a baby in Bethlehem.

We were very aware that this might be Mark's last Christmas with us and it became hard not to spoil him. We felt the children should all be treated equally, so the girls did well for presents that year as well. Mark was with me when I was buying one of Louise's presents, a large very wrinkly, velvet glove puppet dog. When he saw the 'Wrinkles' he fell in love with it and asked for one for himself. I told him I didn't need any more suggestions from him and had already bought his presents. Innocently he asked could he have one next year. He was quite prepared to wait. Of course, I returned to the shop another day and Mark had his 'Wrinkles' for Christmas.

The girls broke up from school, the decorations went up, cards were sent, and Christmas was upon us. Mark was very excited and I was afraid he wouldn't sleep but eventually, after his stocking had been hung up and some mince pies for Father Christmas had been left on the hearth, he was in bed and asleep. Stockings filled and all the preparations done, I was able to go and enjoy the peace of the midnight communion service. Despite Mark's uncertain future it seemed right to offer prayers of thanks that he was there to share that Christmas with us.

We spent a quiet Christmas Day together as a family, my mother having gone to Suffolk. We would join the rest of the family for a couple of days on Boxing Day. It was good to be in church that Christmas morning. We sat near the front and Mark spent a lot of the service playing on the carpet with a small polystyrene aeroplane that Father Christmas had put in his stocking. He had a wonderful day, even seeming better than he had been for some time. He was chattier than of late and very excited although he seemed to move about much more on all fours now. Crawling hadn't been a stage of his recovery, but as his legs weakened he used it to move around. He told me he crawled because his legs felt weak. His balance wasn't so good and he tended to fall over easily.

On the journey on Boxing Day I had time to think. I realized how scared I was about the future. I couldn't pretend things were normal. Tears started to come easily. The rest of Christmas was something of a nightmare. I was so frightened for Mark. Seeing him with Katie and Jake only heightened my awareness of how much he now couldn't do. I must have spoiled the holiday for everyone by being so miserable. Mark, however, seemed to enjoy himself and his presents. The high spot of the stay for him was going for a walk when he took it in turns with Katie and Jake to have rides on Gremlin. But, here again, I could see his deterioration. I needed to hold him on, and when the pony trotted Mark couldn't control his head and stop it bouncing up and down. I felt it couldn't be doing him any good at all, so I kept the walk fairly gentle but he had fun and laughed a lot.

I was glad to be home. Christmas for me had been largely a disaster. Christmas Day at home had been quite pleasant but on the whole my anxiety was so all-consuming it ruined everything.

Two days later Mark suddenly cried out and seemed to collapse. He was holding the back of his neck, obviously in a great deal of pain. I tried not to be too alarmed and considered such innocent explanations as a pulled muscle but nevertheless rang the doctor. He came as soon as he could and we both agreed to wait a little before rushing off to Oxford. As the afternoon progressed Mark seemed very ill, I even thought he might die. Derek told me afterwards that he hadn't feared that then but felt that this might be the beginning of the end. Later that afternoon, although I knew I could go to Oxford whenever I was worried, the doctor rang the hospital and told them we were on our way.

We were met at the door and taken straight into the X-ray department for a scan. The results of this were enough to convince them that they wanted to do a contrast scan in the morning. I could either take him home and come back or stay in hospital with him. I knew I wouldn't sleep at home so we stayed. By now Mark was much better and once settled into bed in the ward was quite active. The next morning he had to have an intravenous needle inserted for the contrast, but this time there was a difference. Magic Cream! They had started to use a lignocaine cream, which, put on the skin for at least an hour, made it so numb the needle didn't hurt. Mark was told a story about Herbie the hedgehog who lost his spines and had to have them put back in, and the Magic Cream stopped it hurting. The badge he was given to wear said 'I'm as brave as Herbie'. Although

Mark never liked the thought of the needle, after that, so long as the cream had had time to work, these occasions weren't quite so bad. As always Mark was well behaved and kept still for the scan, and we returned to the ward to wait for the results. Eventually the doctor appeared, asking to speak to us both. By then Mark was not in any mood to be left, so I went into the office alone.

I was warned by his approach that the news was not good. It was devastating. The tumour was growing again and spreading. The sudden pain was probably the result of a small haemorrhage in the tumour area. There was now no question but that Mark would die. Whatever treatment they did would be only palliative. They would do what they could to maintain Mark's quality of life but they could not cure him.

Given no hope, at that time I didn't want him to live long. I didn't want them to do a myelogram, as they wished. Why should he suffer that? I increased his steroids that night as instructed, but with reluctance. Perhaps I feared the suffering to us in waiting for his death and wanted the 'bad thing' over as soon as possible, perhaps I didn't want Mark to suffer any longer than necessary, perhaps I felt that whatever life he now lived would be futile, to no purpose, now that the 'death sentence' had been passed. How wrong I was proved to be as in the last months of Mark's life we saw him mature, grow and achieve so much in both his own life and those of others! Many have told me since his death of the witness that he and I were during his illness. If he had died then we would never have witnessed the wonderful blossoming of his faith in Jesus as his personal saviour and friend, and his preparation to be with him in heaven.

We came back to Maidenhead, told my mother the news, collected the girls from Celia, and went into town as Mark wanted to go to McDonald's. We were dazed with the first horror of grief. I was totally unable to eat. My throat was constricted, I felt physical pain in it. Tears came easily and frequently in those first few days. It was New Year's Eve. I felt that if anyone wished me a Happy New Year I would scream. Once Mark was in bed and asleep we told the girls. We wanted them to be informed at all stages. It was very necessary for their own coming to terms with the situation, would help their attitude to Mark, and prevent them doing something they might regret. However, they were sworn to secrecy. At that stage we didn't want Mark to find out he was going to die.

That evening I sat in a daze, the cups of coffee the girls made mounted up beside me untouched. I thought I would never laugh again. But amidst all my grief I was aware of a feeling of immense relief. The worry was gone; my worst fears were realized and there was no need to worry any more.

The next morning was worse. Mark was still with us. We had started to grieve for the loss of a life that was still being lived. This made it more difficult as we had to carry on as normal. Mark seemed quite bright and talked gaily about the future. Now Christmas was over he planned which Easter egg he would like and told us that like Louise when he was nine he would open a Piggy Bank account at the National Westminster Bank. We didn't expect him to still be with us for Easter, let alone when he was nine, but we kept up the pretence. It is significant in Mark's acceptance of his death that in later months he never mentioned more than the immediate future.

Although living near to Windsor, we had never been to the Safari Park. It was always one of those things we would do another year. Now, with yesterday's news so fresh, we decided to spend at least some of the bank holiday there.

The first enclosure contained giraffes and zebras. Last night I had thought I would never laugh again. Now as we slowed down while a zebra crossed in front of us Derek commented: 'It's a zebra crossing!' We all collapsed with laughter and I knew that life could become fun again. In that laughter was a small crumb of healing.

Because Mark wanted to play with Edward we spent the afternoon with his family and broke the news to Celia and Rob. Elizabeth was very uncomfortable in Catherine's presence without being allowed to confide in her and we had to permit her to tell Catherine whilst swearing her too to secrecy. Elizabeth needed a confidante of her own, although this proved to be almost an unfair strain on Catherine. That day, not content with lunch at McDonald's in Windsor, Mark wanted to go to McDonald's in Maidenhead for tea. The increase in steroids had actually made him seem quite well that day and his appetite was much better. This was very much his 'McDonald's fad', and over that weekend we were there nearly every day! We had no choice but to give in to these fads; if we didn't he simply didn't eat. It was not a case of holding out and being firm. Although with steroid increases he ate more his appetite was never normal and he had to be coaxed to eat.

That evening I was able to spend some time with Peter. I was grateful that he was giving up time with his family at New Year to see me but this was an example of the support he offered to our whole family throughout Mark's illness. During chats like this with him he always made me cry but I usually felt better afterwards. I always find it helpful to talk with him. I was beginning to feel stronger about the whole situation. 'I dare say I'll survive', was my parting comment to Peter. 'Oh, you'll survive!' was his reply.

The next morning we were again at the Radcliffe. Adrian arrived and explained his reasons for wanting the myelogram. If it showed tumour on the spinal chord they could irradiate that area and possibly increase Mark's mobility and this was worth while. I told him how I felt about not prolonging things. He estimated Mark's life to be a few weeks, maybe months and told us that usually parents appreciate that extra time.

Mark seemed quite well again after Tuesday's episode but since then his right leg was stiff for the first time, even worse than the left, and consequently his walking was worse. The myelogram was carried out under general anaesthetic so we stayed in hospital over night. The myelogram however, showed no tumour in the spine. Adrian suggested that they leave Mark for a few weeks, reassess him at the end of January and decide what, if anything, to do.

Although seeming quite well and recovered from the myelogram, over the weekend Mark was soon complaining of headaches which couldn't be controlled with pain killers. It was the pain which commonly occurs after a myelogram. All we could do was keep him flat and it was several days before he started to get better. I thought he might die, and when I saw the possibility of the few weeks Adrian had promised us slipping away I suddenly realized how much I wanted them. Eventually the headaches dispersed and Mark was able to return to his hour a day at school. Fortunately this was the only time in all Mark's illness that he suffered severe head pain.

I was surprised to discover that despite the fact that time with Mark was limited I didn't feel the need to be with him all the time and still valued time spent either alone, with Derek, or the girls or friends. Sometimes since Mark has died I have wondered that I didn't want to spend every available moment with him, but I obviously needed the breaks and it was probably only through those times away that I was able to keep going as long as necessary.

As January progressed I experienced a deepening sense of peace. I went to the Wives Group New Years party and was surprised to find I could enjoy myself and I also experienced the tremendous benefit of talking to friends. I have learned to share my problems much more during Mark's illness and our bereavement, and have realized the advantages of being able to talk a problem through. It was a tremendous relief not to worry any more. I committed Mark totally into God's care. People suggested that no mother ever completely gives up hope but I am sure I had. It was almost easier to cope with that way. The Sunday after the myelogram I had felt unable to face a normal Sunday morning service and had gone to the early communion service. The next week I went in the evening to the annual covenant service held each new year in the Methodist church. The service held a new meaning for me that year as I spoke the words re-dedicating myself to God: 'I am no longer my own, but yours. Put me to what you will; put me to doing, put me to suffering . . . I freely and wholeheartedly yield all things to your pleasure and disposal . . . you are mine and I am yours.' My whole situation was in God's hands.

I was finding a deep spiritual benefit through taking communion regularly and again, as in August, I was feeling that inflowing of peace and strength due to the many people upholding us in their prayers.

Once again friends rallied round to offer help. Real help is gained not from a friend who says 'What can I do to help? but from the friend who sees a need and does something about it. One such example was Gill. Not a close friend at that time, but a member of the church, she offered to do my ironing, wouldn't take 'No' for an answer, and regularly turned up twice a week for the rest of Mark's life to collect and deliver the ironing. I felt quite guilty because I hate ironing and felt I was using Mark as a good excuse, but it was a lesson for me in learning how to be served by others. In the past I had told others that it was as much a service to God to be the recipient of help from others as to be the helper. I was now learning this experience first hand. As a bonus I have gained a good friend.

Having recovered from the myelogram headaches, Mark had remained quite stable throughout January and the time soon came round for the clinic. David inserted the needle into Mark's vein for the contrast scan, painlessly thanks to magic cream, and Mark showed him the photographs of the hospital Christmas party, again bemoaning the fact that David hadn't been there and telling him how Father Christmas had known his name. David and I had difficulty keeping straight faces. This was the last occasion on which David was Mark's doctor. After six months in neurosurgery he was now moving to a different department, but would still be around. David confided in me the bond he had felt with Mark as his first seriously ill child after starting in that department, and how the job had depressed him at times. He certainly gave all of himself in the care of his patients and their families.

In the clinic Peter Teddy and Adrian told me that the scan had revealed a different state of affairs from that supposed. They now believed what they had previously thought to be the tumour regrowing was a cyst forming on the degenerative tumour tissue. This cyst might carry on filling or might be reabsorbed. The news seemed marvellous to me but I was warned not to raise my hopes too much. That was an impossible warning. Of course I raised my hopes. Whether the error in interpreting the scan was, as the doctors suggested, that on the previous scan what appeared to be metastases were in fact specks of blood that had now disappeared or whether Mark was healed of these secondary growths I don't know, but it seemed to me a miraculous turn of events. Further encouragement was the next clinic appointment. Not for another two months!

For several more weeks Mark's condition remained fairly stable and this was probably the most settled time of his illness. Although, if we were honest, he was slowly deteriorating. He seldom walked without help and became unable to swim with his armbands. One day he was distressed to discover he couldn't straighten his fingers.

Mark had by then been ill for six months and we were entitled to apply for mobility allowance and attendance allowance. Mark was assessed by a doctor and awarded the allowance. Financially this made a great difference as we had found it very expensive having a handicapped child; apart from anything else we used the car so much more.

During this relatively stable time half-term came and we were able to visit Mark's godparents for a couple of days, went swimming and got Mark afloat again with arm bands and rubber ring, went ice skating and on an Awayday by train to Plymouth to visit an elderly friend.

As well as the things we were able to do with Mark, we were overwhelmed by the generosity shown by other people, and during this time of comparative stability he enjoyed some wonderful treats.

In January Derek's brother had invited Mark to visit the control tower at Heathrow airport, where he works, then to be driven round the airfield to see the planes and finally to the Concorde hanger and the chance to sit in the cockpit. That night he had trouble sleeping. 'I'm so excited thinking about all those aeroplane's, he told me. That visit also sparked off a whole new realm of play as he started to play 'offices', being Uncle Dennis in his airport office.

Inspired by Mark's enjoyment of this day, Peter Hudson arranged with a member of another church in our circuit for

Mark to have a flight in the cockpit of a Boeing 757. Mark had never flown before and was thrilled. As we climbed to our cruising altitude and left the clouds behind our progress over the ground below seemed quite slow. 'Ask him to go faster!' said Mark. We were cruising at 600 mph! By this time muscles in Mark's face had weakened and his face did not express his delight so I do hope that Captain Fulton and his crew realized just how much Mark enjoyed the trip.

A ride in a police car prompted Mark's office to become a police office. 'Police' and 'office' were two of the few words he could write without having them spelt out for him. He played at being a policeman. Rolf Harris drew him a special cartoon and there was yet another plane flight, this time in a four-seater.

Mark was still loving school, although he only went part-time, but I was aware that the school was getting concerned about having him. It was a difficult time when I was encouraged to remove him. They seemed to be afraid that he might die at school or in any case were bothered how to explain to the other children when he did die. I was horrified that such fears might rob Mark of the enjoyment school gave him. I was aware of the rights of handicapped children to attend normal schools. There are benefits on both sides and I had already seen how much Mark had to offer the school in the care and friendship the other children showed him; they were honoured to be counted his friends. They have learned many lessons for life through their friendship with Mark.

Adrian and Peter Teddy wrote to the school pleading with them to help make Mark's last months as enjoyable as possible. I felt so strongly against the idea of Mark going to a special school. School for him was being with his friends.

However the school responded wonderfully and instead of having his time reduced Mark started to go for two hours a day and from then on there was never any suggestion of his not going, although at times he became more and more difficult to handle in the classroom. When he was well he enjoyed the company of the other children, at other times he stayed either alone or with one or two other children in the office with the headmistress. He built magnificent models from a construction kit when more able. At other times he lay on a big cushion on the floor and listened to stories. This was such a respite for me, the only time in twenty-four hours when I wasn't on call, an opportunity just to be me for a short while.

His independence was restored by a battery driven red motorbike and soon Mark was the envy of his friends as he drove it around the playground. They loved him to chase them. He was also able to use it when we went shopping, which gave him some freedom from the hated buggy. He could actually 'run' away from me again!

I have often mulled over the problems we experienced with Mark's schooling and wondered if we made the right decisions. Should we have given in and sent him to a special school? Would he have been happier there? Was it a denial on our part to acknowledge that he was different? We so wanted him to be normal, did we try to pretend he was less different than he was? In answer to all these doubts I have come to the conclusion that we took the right course of action, for several reasons. My driving force was Mark's desire to be at school with his friends and to go to the school he had always expected to go to. Alwyn school was part of his life. He had been to the gate twice a day all his life to take and fetch the girls. For my part, if Mark had gone to a special school they would doubtless have taken him for longer hours, even all day, and I would have been denied the many happy hours we spent together during those last months of his life. He was entitled to be at his local infants school and I am very glad we insisted.

Mark was not the only one to gain from this experience. Everyone involved, teachers, pupils and even parents, have, I am sure, learned something from Mark's presence at Alwyn school. After all the problems and difficulties we had overcome, despite all the reservations the school had, Mark had continued at school and the staff had responded to Adrian's request and truly contributed to Mark's happiness in his last months, for which we are grateful.

7

Healing

The time was drawing near for Mark's next hospital appointment. Two months had passed so quickly. It had seemed a stable time, but looking back we realized that Mark had been getting slowly worse. He was completely unable to walk without help. His speech was more difficult to understand and when he was sitting his legs tended to be stiff, his knees and ankles straight. The spasms which caused this also made his hip joint want to straighten, making sitting difficult, he tended to slip off his chair. His most comfortable position was kneeling; when his knees were forced to bend his hips did too.

During this time, in wanting to pursue every avenue I wondered if we should be seeking someone with a ministry of healing to minister to Mark and I began to think and read much more about divine healing.

From the very first days of Mark's illness prayers had been said for his recovery. We were amazed as the months went on how widely the prayer net spread. We prayed for Mark's physical recovery, although knowing that statistically the chances were less than twenty per cent. However, we believed he would regain complete health. It is strange how rarely we hear prayers said in public places specifically for healing. For strength and support – yes – but not often for healing. Is this because many do not actually believe this will happen and are reluctant to ask God for what they don't think will be granted or be able to be granted? My mother was told it was wrong to pray for healing, it was asking God to change his mind! After Mark had died people who we knew had prayed for us all passed comments such as, 'We all knew it had to end like this sometime.' However, *we* believed much of the time that he would get better and we attempted to pass this positive attitude to Mark.

After Mark was diagnosed terminal on New Years Eve I was without hope for a few weeks, committing Mark totally to God, but when the diagnosis was reviewed my hopes soared and my prayers for his healing became as fervent as ever.

My thoughts about healing concern the whole person. Divine healing need not necessarily involve the curing of an ailment, but a healing of mind and spirit to cope with that condition. A heart, mind and spirit that accepts whatever may happen to the body in a sense of peace and trust in God is a healed person, but at the time I looked for total healing for Mark. Friends talked to me about taking more positive steps. Should they be obeying the commands of James and come and lay hands on Mark and anoint him with oil? I was not enthusiastic about anything that might be something of a strange ordeal for Mark, and I believe that James was instructing the people of his day to use the treatments of the time in a prayerful way. I believe God heals today through the skills of doctors and nurses and modern technology. I believe he heals through radio-therapy. I was given a booklet to read which I found hard to cope with and which I decided to ignore, as I felt the guilt it could impose could be dangerous. It suggested that God chose whom of the sick he would heal according to their faith.

At this point I was in a state of some confusion about the whole subject. I felt that so many were praying for Mark that this should be enough. Peter called to see us one day and I asked him his views. I think his thoughts on healing were much along the same lines as my own. He feels that our prayers at communion bring perhaps the greatest benefit to those we pray for. The whole subject of intercessory prayer is a mystery. I cannot think that God needs us to draw his attention to those in need of help or to enable him to grant what we pray for, but more that in our prayer we are sharing in God's love and care of all creation and so entering into the mystery. I cannot believe that God cares any less for someone if we forget to pray for them or for whom there is no one to pray than for a Christian surrounded by other praying Christians. Yet I can still witness to the feeling of being upheld by prayer and to the power of prayer.

Mark was by this time regularly attending communion services for blessing. At the time we were unaware that we were witnessing the very beginnings of his deepening relationship with Jesus and of a growing faith and spirituality unusual in children. He had always been to Sunday School, said his prayers and enjoyed Bible stories but over the months we were to see his faith become deeply personal. This had started when, no longer wanting to go to Sunday School, he preferred to come to church with me. During a communion service I explained what we were doing and asked if he wanted to be blessed. He had become so reserved I expected him to refuse and was delighted when, such was his enthusiasm that I had to stop him crawling forward with every row of communicants! 'Why did he like communion so much?' I asked. 'I like the words Peter Hudson says', he answered: 'God bless you Mark, Jesus is with you.'

After our talk Peter told me about the Revd Christopher Johnson, then the vicar of Eton, who has a healing ministry. I telephoned and he asked to see Derek and me alone first:

we should be at peace before we returned at another time with Mark. The parents' influence and attitude can be very influential in the healing of a child. Peter came with us to see Christopher Johnson. We talked briefly of Mark's problem, admitting that he had deteriorated since the last hospital visit, which suggested that the cyst was slowly enlarging.

One at a time Derek and I lay on his couch while Christopher Johnson laid hands on us (one on the head and one on our hands) and prayed. I found it a moving experience tempered by strangeness. I didn't relax completely as I was fighting tears and for some reason didn't want to let them go because I felt some reserve – not usually a problem! I think that had I repeated this experience I would have relaxed completely but this was the only time, as in future Mark was the 'patient'.

Following this visit, for a short time I found it very difficult to cope with the fact of Mark's illness. This was the only time I felt so self-centred and sorry for myself. 'Why should this have happened to me, keeping me confined, caring for a handicapped, sick child, who should have started school last September and freed me for the first time in eleven years to think of my own life, career etc.?' (This does not mean that I hadn't greatly enjoyed being at home with my children, but I had been expecting that phase of my life to be drawing naturally to a close.) At that time I did not think of Mark's suffering, only my own. I felt very low and depressed, and not a bit peaceful following Christopher Johnson's prayers. It seemed as though these negative feelings were a direct result of the visit, almost as though you have to get worse before you get better. Fortunately it didn't last long. Three times in as many days in different places and circumstances I read or heard part of Luke 9, where Jesus tells us to take up our cross daily and follow him. I suddenly realized I was trying so hard to put down my 'cross' and that I was building up resentment within myself. This revelation completely removed all these feelings and I felt at peace.

A week later we returned to Eton with Mark. He and I had talked about the coming visit and how the minister we were going to see would ask Jesus to make him better. *I believed it.* So did Mark. Would he be able to walk that afternoon, he asked. On another occasion he asked me when he would be able to run like Edward and before I could answer said 'I don't mind if I can't run if I can only walk.' One evening he chose a prayer from his book which gave thanks for being able to run, jump and play. He couldn't walk, let alone run or jump. I was reluctant to read it for him, but he insisted and eventually, upset, I asked if he really wanted to give thanks for these things. 'I can do them a little bit, I can crawl' he said, so we adapted the prayer and gave thanks for the abilities he had. It was a humbling experience!

Mark took to Mr Johnson straight away. Although he was usually warm and friendly to the few people he was close to, since his illness he'd become very reserved with those he didn't know and I was surprised to see him open up and chat about his favourite toys and promise to bring one next time. In fact this was the only visit he really chatted, because his speech had deteriorated a lot by the next. He contentedly reclined on the couch with my arm behind him and with Derek by the bed we were all united in a circle. Without a great deal of preamble Mr Johnson laid his hands on Mark's head and began to pray at great length. Mark remained silent and still throughout – some feat for a five-year-old, even a sick one! This was a further insight into Mark's awakening faith. Christopher Johnson sensed a great peace in Mark, and Mark told us later how he had liked Mr

Johnson. I am sure this was because Christopher Johnson seemed to us a very spiritual person and Mark sensed it too.

The next day, a Saturday, was a beautiful early spring day. Mark got up in excellent spirits. He was tremendously happy, cheerful and outgoing all that day and thoroughly enjoyed going to a friend's birthday party in the afternoon dressed as a pirate. It is a day that sticks out clearly in my memory, a day to treasure. I credited the previous day's happenings for it. But on the Sunday suddenly Mark couldn't walk at all. I had to carry him into church and to the communion rail. The next two days were worse, he was terribly miserable and didn't go to school. At the time I didn't refer to his worsened state, in case I should draw his attention to it. As if he didn't know! Now I wish I had sympathized more, but maybe my attitude in some way encouraged his tremendous fighting spirit! However, he knew, and was extremely difficult because of it.

I was relieved that we were due at the clinic. That scan confirmed my suspicions that the cyst was significantly larger, but I didn't worry too much. I felt sure they would drain it as Mr Teddy had suggested. There was nothing to lose. However, Mr Teddy wasn't there and Adrian felt that Mark's chances of surviving surgery were so slim they would not attempt it. He estimated his life to be about two months and warned that he would gradually become more sleepy, as the cyst pressed on the reticular area of the brain, the part responsible for waking and sleeping, and he would eventually slip into a coma. I asked if an increase in steroids would help. Adrian thought not as we were dealing with a cyst not a tumour, but said I could double them twice but no more.

I was devastated. The shock was so great. I was so sure they would do something. I sat in the consulting room and cried and cried. It must have been the only time when I was really upset at the hospital. Eventually I left. The tears had been therapeutic and I arrived home much more in control to break the news to Derek. He seemed to take it surprisingly calmly and left soon after to play badminton as planned, but a friend who saw him that evening told me how upset he was and how badly he played. He went hoping to work out his feelings on the shuttlecock but didn't play well enough to achieve anything!

I spent much of the evening on the phone to both Peter and Christopher Johnson. Christopher Johnson's attitude was that, as with me, this deterioration was not unexpected as we had taken the positive step of seeking healing. All we could do was place Mark entirely in God's hands. He also strongly recommended against the possibility of chemotherapy, which Adrian had offered if we wanted it. Adrian didn't think it would help but the decision was ours. We agreed with Christopher Johnson. It might seem strange that in a life and death issue we considered Mark's distress if he lost his hair – his cherished curls – but it seemed an unnecessary affront to his dignity when it almost certainly would not help.

It is difficult to describe my feelings the next day. I awoke feeling on top of the world. It would have been so easy then to give in and accept Mark's death, easier in fact than to fight but fight I would. However at least I could see an end. Mark would recover or he would die. My fear had been years of caring for a handicapped child. I am not proud of that fear but how I now admire those people who are in that situation! I prayed fervently for Mark's healing. God's peace was very real to me.

Looking back I realized that during the past weeks and particularly at that time Jesus had been slowly and steadily filling me with his spirit, not as a sudden, memorable experience but slowly, drop by drop, until I became aware of the joy and delight in my life which words can hardly describe, there in the midst of all the sadness and grief of the situation I was experiencing. A feeling I can only describe as like falling in love!

Prayers for Mark's recovery were as fervent as ever and several people observed a day of fasting and prayer for healing, which was all a great encouragement to me not to give in and accept Mark's death. However, as the weeks went on and Mark deteriorated, beginning to be sleepy as Adrian foretold, I realized that hope was fading and being replaced by an acceptance of his death.

A few days after that clinic appointment came Mothering Sunday. Elizabeth had taken Mark to buy me a New Testament and he had written in it. Over recent weeks I had been reading the Bible more than ever before. Mark liked me to sit with him until he went to sleep. This had first started in January. I knew I was setting a precedent but how could I refuse? How could I have lived with myself if he had died in the night? I spent this time every night reading the Bible, no doubt also a silent witness to Mark. Many passages gave me great comfort and help, particularly amongst the psalms. My handbag-sized New Testament could now be with me always. When I was in hospital with Mark it was sometimes all I had to read, but it was more than enough!

As Easter approached, Mark's physical condition worsened further but despite frustrations, tantrums and miseries at times, I can only think back to that Easter as a happy time. The weather alone was enough to lift the spirits, although fine weather can have the opposite effect if you are low. Mark was at his best in the evenings. When he slept during the day evening became for a short while a cherished family time. He particularly enjoyed helping Derek count the day's takings! At bedtime I often had long chats with him. We read stories of Easter and Holy Week.

His favourite was the story of the risen Jesus appearing to Mary in the garden. He got so excited as the point approached where Jesus spoke her name. How could she not recognize Jesus? Edward came to stay one night and Mark insisted I read this story to him, Mark as usual hooting with laughter at Mary thinking Jesus was the gardener.

I read the story of the Last Supper and Mark immediately recognized that it was 'like communion'. I used this to build on to Peter's suggestion that he might like to take communion. His first answer was 'no', mostly because he was 'off' bread at the time. I let the subject drop. During Holy Week we celebrated a Passover meal at the Ladies luncheon club of which I was secretary. We had bought some lovely crusty granary loaves for it. Mark enjoyed the meal and the bread, was aware that we had been celebrating a form of communion, and on the way home asked if he could take communion on Easter Sunday.

Derek and I had decided that we would not increase Mark's steroids if it was unlikely to help, but one evening I heard him cry and rushed in to find he was biting his finger. He had been sucking it and his jaw had clenched, he couldn't release his finger. This frightened us and the next day I doubled his dose but it had a very transient effect, giving only one day when he seemed a little better so that we wished we hadn't bothered. His hand was now too weak to write and he could only open his mouth a little. He became very upset one day when he couldn't even open his mouth wide enough to take a bite of choc ice.

Easter Sunday brought with it the new Bible Mark had requested and lots of Easter eggs. He unwrapped them all and seemed to enjoy playing with them much more than eating them. We went to church, Mark looking forward to taking communion. Peter, with roving microphone in hand, introduced the song 'Lord of the Dance' and said that it was a certain little boy's favourite, was that right Mark? Mark's giggle over the loudspeaker delighted everyone. We've got the song on tape and he often wanted it played. He remembered singing it and dancing round the church with the rest of the beginners department of the Sunday School the previous June during the Anniversary service. Mark had asked me to take the bread and wine in communion for him but when we knelt altogether as a family a little hand reached up over the rail for his own share in the 'body and blood of Christ', understanding it as an expression of shared love between Jesus and himself. A wonderful moment.

On Monday afternoon we went for a walk with friends. Mark was by now too weak to drive his motorbike and he hated the buggy. The result was that I carried him nearly everywhere we went, but he had lost so much weight he was not very heavy. That evening we shared a Chinese take-away meal. Mark was having difficulty eating and chewing and tended to push food into his mouth. He choked on a piece of meat. I tried to put my fingers in his mouth to remove it and his jaw clamped down on them in a spasm. I couldn't do anything but turn him upside down while be bit my fingers! He was quite blue. I felt calm and a certain resignation as it was happening but at the same time prayed 'Not like this – please.' Suddenly the obstruction was gone. Mark pointed to his throat and then his stomach saying, 'It's gone from here to here!'

There were bad times over Easter but they are blotted out by the memory of an all-pervading peace at that time. I acknowledge for Mark and all of us a healing in spirit and a great closeness with God. I cannot help but compare with the previous Christmas when I was so overwhelmed with my fears for Mark that it was a miserable time. Throughout Mark's illness and death and all the ups and downs I found, as in so many things in life, that the fear and worry was the most destroying. Once something was a fact it was easier to cope with.

8

Back to Hospital

Mark was by now very ill. He slept for much of every day, often asleep in my lap in the garden as the weather was unseasonably warm, although he still woke very early in the mornings. Breakfast television was a great help, as he would happily watch from my bed while I came to more slowly! At this time his speech was very indistinct and he could no longer crawl or write. On the whole his quality of life was poor.

The weekend after Easter we had our one and only bad hospital experience. It could have been avoided, as subsequently Mr Teddy made it quite clear to all his staff that there was a bed at the Radcliffe whenever Mark needed it for whatever reason. The trouble arose because it was at a weekend when Mark began to suffer from urine retention. The duty registrar at the Radcliffe was unaware of our clearance to go at any time and we were shunted to a local hospital which had no medical notes and didn't understand his condition. It was the cause of unnecessary distress and dangers.

The following Tuesday we returned for our next clinic appointment. Mr Teddy saw how ill and miserable Mark was. He appreciated the problems he was having with swallowing and passing urine and to my amazement announced that Mark's quality of life was so poor he would operate: there was nothing to lose. We stayed in hospital, as the operation was planned for Friday. Being in hospital was a great respite, making me aware of the strain of caring for Mark at home, but also I realized, back in the hospital environment, how much more easily I coped with him compared with the previous summer.

We were warned that the operation would be extremely risky. I spent the next two days very aware that they might be the last of Mark's life. We walked into Oxford and bought a birthday card for Edward, who would be six the next Monday and I helped Mark write it. Would he still be alive by Edward's birthday?

I explained to Mark that he was going to have an operation. He asked to see Peter, who came, stayed a while, and prayed with him. I was beginning to realize how fond of Peter Mark was. He loved to see him, and Peter was one of the few people Mark would happily go to. It was only later that I discovered how much the friendship was mutual and how Peter loved Mark.

I sat up late that Thursday night. Eventually I went to bed and lay reading the Bible Mark had given me. In the book of Acts I read: 'Stretch out your hand to heal, and grant that wonders and miracles may be performed through the name of your holy Servant Jesus', and made the prayer my own.

By nine o'clock once again I was carrying Mark to the operating theatre. We settled down to wait. We had been told to expect about an hour and a half in theatre. Mark should be back by midday after a time in recovery. This time came and went as we waited for news. We drank countless cups of coffee and tea punctuated by visits to the loo! It was lunchtime when Mr Teddy came into the ward. He had probed as deep as he dared and not found the cyst. They had scanned Mark and found that he had missed by only a millimetre or two. They were planning to give Mark further anaesthesia and attempt to drain the cyst from the outside whilst it was under the scan. We settled to wait again but at least felt free to leave the ward for a few minutes to have something to eat and phone home with the news. I realized I must be getting used to this – the summer before I couldn't have eaten under such circumstances!

Eventually, six hours after Mark had left the ward, we were asked to go and fetch him. It was unusual for parents to be invited to go into the recovery room but Mark was asking for us and it had been a very long operation!

Mr Teddy came to see him and pronounced the operation a success. They had aspirated about twenty-five ml of fluid from the cyst. Mark had survived beyond all expectation and made a rapid recovery, not even needing intensive therapy. Immediately we noticed how much clearer Mark's speech was, and the nurses could understand him now. He could open his mouth wide. Mr Teddy came to see him every day, one day bringing his little boy Alex. I could see what he meant about them being alike. On another occasion I returned from getting Mark a drink to find him deep in conversation with Mr Teddy all about 'He-Man' and 'Thundercats' and whatever other toys both he and Alex, in common with most little boys, enjoyed playing with at that time.

Monday was Bank Holiday and Una came to see him. Mark had just discovered to his great delight that he could write again and developed a great enthusiasm for making lists. He copied out his fluid chart, and made lists of all the nasty things that happened to him like 'operation' and 'drip', but best of all was the list of the food he wanted for his birthday party, now only six weeks away.

He was able to sit up well, his legs were no longer stiff, and his feet rested easily on the foot rest of the buggy. Two days later after I had dressed him in the morning he slipped to the floor from the side of the bed and took a few steps with help, the first for at least a month.

I truly believed that God was healing through the changing attitudes of the doctors in deciding to operate and through their skill. The success of the operation and Mark's rapid recovery were answers to prayer. Mark believed it too. 'Was it God or Jesus that made me better?' he asked! I read from Isaiah: 'The people who walked in darkness have seen a great light . . . You have given them great joy, Lord; you have made them happy . . . You have broken the yoke that burdened them.' I was effusive in my praise and thanks.

The yoke was soon to burden me again. Even before we left hospital I was suspecting that Mark was not as well as he had been, but tried to ignore it and hoped it was my imagination. Back home he was so much better. The physiotherapist provided him with a walking frame and he began to learn to walk again, but his enthusiasm was waning. I realized I was not imagining it, he was getting worse again, and quickly. In less than a month the cyst had refilled.

It was half-term, the girls were away for a few days leaving us alone with Mark. He began to be sleepy again and deteriorated so much over the weekend that I rang the hospital. I told Peter, who suggested to me for the first time that Mark understood the situation and that we should be positive about preparing him for his death, but that it was not time yet and he was not going to give up hope yet. I felt strengthened and ready for what the next day might bring and from then on we began to be a little less discrete with Mark about the nature of his illness and he began to demand more knowledge. On one occasion after a scan he asked what Mr Teddy had said. I told him he had said we could go home, 'No, what did Mr Teddy say?' he demanded. And later I started to tell him about the 'thing' in his head which made him so ill.

A scan revealed the refilled cyst. Mr Teddy said they would drain it once more, under scan. The same risks applied. As the aspiration was to take place in the scan room I told Mark he was only having a scan. It was a silly thing to do. When he came round from the anaesthetic and found himself in the recovery room he thought he'd had an operation and he was furious. I promised always to tell him the truth in future. His voice was loud and clear, not even a hint of the nasal twang it had at even the best times. He recovered immediately from the anaesthetic, was chatty and noisy, the nurses had never seen him like it, and he was able to go home the next day. We had a wonderful weekend. By the next day his voice was already less clear and I suspected the improvement would not last long. But whatever the future might bring it could not take away the joy of that weekend. He was almost running as he held my hand, lacking only the confidence to let go. He took communion again the next day, walking to the rail with help. How I cherished that weekend. For the first time in his illness I was really living only for today. I thought I had before but I really knew it this time. 'Take no thought for the morrow . . .' So easy to say, so difficult to do, but for that weekend I really made it!

As I suspected, by Monday there was definite deterioration and within a fortnight he was very ill again. It may, with hindsight, have been not altogether kind to Mark to give him back so much only to have it removed so quickly. He had to come to terms with losing his skills very quickly and it made him miserable. He was having physiotherapy three times a week and was back at school but as he deteriorated they found they couldn't keep him in the classroom. He could no longer sit comfortably on a chair and once again was most comfortable kneeling. As before, he hated the buggy and wanted to be carried everywhere.

Within a fortnight a scan revealed that the tumour was now growing again. However there was still a suggestion of some further treatment. Adrian and Mr Teddy were discussing a new method of injecting radioactive particles into the cyst. I talked with the registrar, who held similar views to Peter. He felt that Mark, who was not stupid, must appreciate something of the nature of his illness and had a right to know. Peter had told me there were various stories that explain death to children, usually comparing death and new life to metamorphosis.

That middle weekend in June brought with it both the school fun day and the Church Anniversary, both painful reminders of the previous year when all had been well. I remembered other school events in the past and how Mark would have been running about with the other children. I felt physical pain at the memory. At that time seeing Mark unable to run around as he would wish was more painful than the fact of his coming death.

Since Easter we had seen more signs of Mark's spiritual growth. His favourite stories were Bible stories and at bedtime he would have no other read to him. One day he put on one side all his 'Jesus books', as he called them, with the words 'These are the only stories I've got to have.' When Gill was visiting one day she tried to tidy them away and was severely told off! Mark often 'took' me to our local Christian bookshop to add to his collection. His Bible, a hymn book (singing Bible!), a service book (praying Bible!), his children's prayer book and lots of children's story books about Jesus and other Bible characters, books about modern day characters or animals which reflected Christian ideas and attitudes – the books were really so precious that as he became more ill and spent time in my bed, all had to be moved with him and be wherever he was. Sharing these stories and our prayer time together each day was a very special time for Mark and me as we were both nurtured in our faith, Mark's own example being an inspiration to me.

9

Birthday

In January we didn't expect Mark to live until his sixth birthday in June. After the revised diagnosis in February we began to hope that he might, but our hope diminished and when at the end of March the prognosis was two months we didn't expect it at all.

Now, after the success of his operation, suddenly his birthday seemed a reality. In hospital he started making lists of the food he wanted for the party on the computer with Una. We began to plan a big party for all his and our many friends who had drawn so close to us over the months of difficulty. The guest list grew, old friends, friends from the church, Sue, Una and David as well as some of the nurses from the hospital.

With adults and children the guest list was approaching eighty. Invitations went out and were nearly all accepted. The party was planned for the Sunday afternoon after his birthday. Since his little school friends would be lost in such a crowd they were to have a McDonald's party on the day itself.

Mark's sixth birthday, Wednesday 17 June, dawned in a downpour but it couldn't dampen his excitement. Visitors started to arrive before 8.30 am! One friend brought the present Mark had specifically asked for – a little pin-on cross. Derek took the day off, the school allowed the girls to stay home, and for the first time ever we went as a family to see the Royal procession to the Ascot races.

Later in the afternoon we went to McDonald's for Mark's long awaited McDonald's party. I was afraid the day would prove too much but he was in excellent spirits sitting amongst his friends. Refusing my help to eat or drink, he hardly had a thing but enjoyed himself so much. His friends were so important to him, which was one of the reasons he liked school so much and why I fought so hard to keep him there. Edward, Alex, Michael, Jason, Helen and Laura – special friends who were so caring and loving towards him.

We lit the six candles on his cake, iced to look like a giant ice cream, as he had chosen. I had to make two identical cakes, one for his birthday, one for his big party. We sang 'Happy Birthday' and with the help of his sisters and friends Mark blew out the candles – blowing wasn't easy.

But the next day we were back at the Radcliffe. Mark was so much worse that I had rung Mr Teddy, who asked to see him. He was so weak during the morning as he waited for his scan that he couldn't even press the buttons on his new transformers which made the heads shoot off. Probably he was very tired after his birthday, for when Mr Teddy came to see him suddenly he was able to do it and showed off to him. The nurses produced a big strawberry and cream gateau with birthday candles on it and sang 'Happy Birthday' again. Mr Teddy asked us to come into hospital the next Wednesday for the new treatment.

As the days went by I had been preparing food for the party. I hadn't catered on this scale since before Mark was ill and enjoyed the planning and preparation. Mark, excited and looking forward to his party, was happy to sit with Gran for stories and games while I was working, but I found that I spent almost as much time with him as usual.

On Sunday morning in the rush of preparations my eyes

fell on one of the Torquay pottery motto plates in our collection. 'Don't spoil today's blue skies with tomorrow's clouds.' That was my thought for the day! Whatever the next days and weeks might bring we would and did enjoy that day. Friends were marvellous in their assistance to make this a day to remember. During the party they saw to it that I was free to enjoy the event.

Soon the afternoon was upon us and guests started to arrive laden with presents we hadn't expected them to bring. This was our thank you to everyone. Mark knelt on the floor playing with some of his new toys and when David the doctor arrived he was pleasantly surprised to find Mark much better than he had expected. As the afternoon wore on the food gradually disappeared. Once again he had lots of help blowing out his candles and in no time at all friends were leaving and I was putting a very tired but happy Mark to bed.

The party over, Mark's thoughts turned more to the impending hospital stay. He was very unhappy about it and was becoming increasingly anxious. I am sure this affected his condition and he was very poorly. He was insisting that he wouldn't have sleeping medicine when he went into hospital and made me write this on the calendar so that I wouldn't forget!

Mark's anxiety built up all Wednesday morning, making him very grumpy, but in the afternoon, bags packed, we were just about to leave for the hospital when they phoned telling us not to come. Mr Teddy no longer felt able to do the operation he had planned. I was given an appointment for the next day to discuss it with him. Mark was very relieved not to be going to hospital, although I felt that he must in some way realize that the operation might have made him better. If so, he might understand what that implied.

Peter Teddy explained that when Adrian had told him exactly what was involved he realized they hadn't the sophisticated equipment needed for the job. It would involve a large number of needles being inserted into the cyst at the same time. He told me that this technique, which originated in Sweden, is carried out in Sheffield. He had telephoned the neurosurgeons in Sheffield and asked if they would operate on Mark, but they had only treated cases similar to his on three occasions and without success. They asked to see Mark's scans but advised that they were most unlikely to decide to go ahead. I would not have wanted to take Mark to Sheffield for such a small chance of success. He would have hated going into a strange hospital where he didn't know anyone and if he died there, as would have been likely, I would have been miles from home and amongst strangers.

We talked around the possibilities of what more could be done for Mark. They could re-aspirate the cyst, but it would only fill up again and anyway the tumour was now growing again. We could continue to increase his steroids, but that would bring with it the voracious appetite he had known the previous year and the subsequent weight gain, and any relief would only be temporary. How much more should Mark be put through? Peter Teddy said that if it was his son he would do no more, and that was my feeling also. He said there was no point in taking Mark back for clinics as he didn't like going but, of course, if we had any problems we could ring or bring him in straight away. If we couldn't cope at home he suggested we enquire about Helen House. He couldn't give me any idea how long Mark would live. I felt very much that it wouldn't be long, not more than a very few weeks. I had been composed throughout the interview. As I rose to leave I felt the tears begin to prick my eyes. Peter Teddy stood up, put his arms around me and cried with me. Mark was so like his son Alex, he said. His tears told me more than words could ever have done. He had tried everything possible and was now with great reluctance having to give up.

Yes, now the 'yoke' was certainly back but Jesus says 'my yoke is easy and my burden is light', and in his strength the yoke was indeed made easier. During Mark's last three months his faith continued to develop. By the time he died he had a close personal friendship with Jesus, who I can only presume had revealed himself to Mark. His spirituality came from within, not from our prompting. I believe he came completely to terms with his death. If only he had been able to talk more easily perhaps he could have told us so much more. Those extra months gained through surgery were important for all of us but not least for Mark's spiritual preparedness to meet Jesus, and we were helped to cope in no small way by Mark's own example as he lived his life closely with Jesus. He and I must have been nurturing each other to a certain extent as through our shared experience I felt my own faith deepening and growing.

I had accepted the news with a certain resignation. After all, this was the third time, but this time there was more finality. Derek, however, took it really badly as if he was at last understanding what it meant. He was still a long way off accepting Mark's death.

In some ways the uncertainty of not knowing how long Mark would live made things harder. That night I didn't know how to pray or what to pray for. As I said the Lord's prayer very slowly I seemed to hear a voice speak the words 'twelve weeks'. I was amazed. Mark could not possibly live another twelve weeks. I didn't believe it. Mark was so ill at that time I almost couldn't face the thought of another three months like it. However by the next morning I found that idea even more entrenched in my mind than if the doctors had given that prognosis. When Mark's health subsequently improved over the next few days I began to believe it to be possible and I became convinced that Mark would die at the end of September. I really believed that God had spoken to me and given me a knowledge that helped me to plan the next few weeks and the summer holidays with confidence.

Mark was very relieved that Peter Teddy had said he didn't have to return to the hospital, and for five days he got better and better. The relief must have been a small part of it but the improvement must have been a consequence of an increase in steroids the previous week in preparation for the treatment he didn't have, and which affected the growing tumour. By the Sunday he was easily pulling himself up into a standing position and was almost our old chatty Mark. We couldn't stop him talking! He was able to play on his own again and his office now became very important. He arranged lots of things on his desk and easily stood up, sat on his chair, and then returned to the floor when he wanted to. He developed a passion for Ferrero Rocher chocolates, and the clear plastic boxes they come in were incorporated into his office, each one containing some item of his office equipment. His office had become well known and he received presents for it both for his birthday and at other times. He spent many happy hours just rearranging things and writing things down. He eagerly sought new equipment, pens, pieces of paper, ink pad and stamper, files and stationery, anything to do with the office. For his birthday someone had given him a writing set including a very fat pen which he found easy to hold and write with even when his hand became quite weak.

The contrast with the previous week was incredible. Only the week before we had been told Mark would definitely die. Now he seemed so well it was impossible to be sad, and we could only be happy at the way he was then.

One evening we went to school to see the slides of Elizabeth's recent school trip to the Isle of Wight. Edward and Mark sat together passing comments and giggling together. A week ago he would have been too ill to go. Now he was chatting, crawling around easily, eating better and altogether much happier. Despite this we made the decision not to increase the steroids again when this effect wore off.

A week after the meeting with Mr Teddy I went to meet Elizabeth from school. Louise had gone to a friend's for tea. As I waited with Mark as usual sitting on my hip suddenly the pressure of his leg on my abdomen became uncomfortable. I got back into the car as the pain started. Elizabeth arrived and we set off for home. I didn't get there! I had to stop the car, afraid I would faint. Fortunately a friend was passing and drove me to the doctor's. Soon Mark was waving me off to hospital in an ambulance, too thrilled that it wasn't him for once to be worried about me!

The diagnosis was an ectopic pregnancy. Fourteen years earlier the same thing had happened: the embryo lodges in a fallopian tube and requires major surgery to be removed. By eight o'clock that night I was in the theatre. I hadn't been planning a pregnancy although I am sure that, knowing the situation with Mark, many people thought I had. At that time I just didn't know whether if Mark died I would want to have another baby. I certainly hadn't before he became ill. The surgeon managed to remove the embryo and leave the tube intact but wasn't sure if it was blocked or not, so he wanted to do a laparoscopy in a few weeks time to look at the tube and if it was damaged, sterilize me.

When Derek came to visit me that night he brought with him a get well message from Mark and also his cross, which he had sent for me and wanted me to wear. He wanted it back, however, and the next day 'took' Derek to the Christian book shop to buy one for me.

The week I spent in hospital was a miserable time. I couldn't wait to get home and be back with Mark. Children under ten were not allowed to visit and even knowing the situation the ward staff were too inflexible to allow Mark in. Fortunately the weather was lovely and once I was up I was able to go outside and see the children. My first visitor had been Peter, and we teased him about having such a problem family to care for!

Mark was quite happy with me in hospital. There couldn't have been a better time in all his illness for me to leave him. He was so well and in such good spirits. I felt a little cheated that I had missed some of that time, but it gave Derek valuable time with him and me some sort of a rest.

Another effect of my illness was in Mark's new consideration for me. I couldn't carry him around so he happily went in the buggy and got very cross when, as I started to regain my strength, I began to lift him occasionally.

At home again I needed constant help. Friends took it in turns to be with me in order to lift Mark when necessary. However, early mornings were a problem. Derek leaves the house before five o'clock and when Mark woke up I would have to wake Elizabeth to come and lift him to the toilet. She was in general very co-operative but after a few weeks, particularly once the holidays had started, became less enthusiastic about being woken so early each morning.

After two or three weeks at home I was for a short time less able to cope emotionally. Mark had got used to going to sleep without me sitting with him. My usual Bible reading time in the day was gone and I had got out of the habit of daily reading. I felt desperately low. Instead of seeking God's help I was trying to cope in my own strength. Realizing this I tearfully poured it all out to him, sought his forgiveness, help and strength, and once again received his peace. Jesus is our saviour, our God and our Lord, but, most important, the very best friend we could ever have. But he won't impose himself upon us, he waits to be asked. I had been forgetting to ask!

Even before I had left hospital I was becoming aware that Mark's incredible improvement was beginning to wear off and that he was also putting on weight, an expected side effect of the steroids. His face slowly became bloated, not as badly as the previous year, but enough for him to look quite different. However he remained in good spirits and that was enough for us.

We all had to be very much on our toes at that time. Any misdemeanour, however small, was recorded in Mark's 'naughty book'. It made very embarrassing reading at times but was also hilarious. No one escaped being commandeered to write down what Mark dictated and also to type the naughty list on to the computer and print it out.

About a month after my operation my health visitor called to see how she might help. It was only then I found out I could have had a nurse in every morning to help with Mark until I could lift him again. It was now too late because Carol was coming at the weekend to help, and the following week Derek would be on holiday. After that I would be able to lift Mark again without difficulty.

The health visitor continued to ask how she could help. I didn't really know, as I hadn't been in that situation before, and she didn't know. Locally, I didn't find anyone experienced in the care of a terminally ill child. The help I could have used was offered too late. I didn't need help nursing Mark, which was what people seemed most to want to offer. There was nothing I couldn't do for him. A mother expects to look after her child and the child expects it too. The care of a child is so different from that of an adult and many medical people have not had training in it. Some areas have a district paediatric nurse who will visit and befriend the family of a dying child and the child himself. Towards the end of Mark's life they suggested a nurse to sit with Mark while I went out for a few hours. I would not have left a fit and healthy six-year-old with a complete stranger, let alone a dying one!

It was only after Mark's death that I could reflect how we might have been better served, but I hadn't realized it at the time. What we had needed was befriending at about the time that we stopped going to Oxford. The hospital had sent through a recommendation to my local practice for a MacMillan nurse, but for some reason they were reluctant to bring in outside help. They felt their practice nurses could cope, but they are not specifically trained in terminal care. If this had happened, by the time Mark died he would have known and probably loved this person, accepted her as a friend rather than as a nurse and been happy to stay with her. Nobody was to blame. We were in a rare situation that few people are equipped to cope with. Inevitably all those involved were affected emotionally by the experience. As it happened, this omission in Mark's care was insignificant because of all the support shown by Peter and our friends from the church. Also David, Una and Sue all continued to visit, telephone and be supportive beyond the call of duty.

10

Summer Holidays

The summer holidays began. Elizabeth spent the first four days at Guide camp and Carol and the children arrived to stay. Mark had been very slowly deteriorating but was still far better than he had been at the time of his birthday.

Once Elizabeth was home we all went to Windsor, Elizabeth and I to buy her school uniform (she was moving on to secondary school in September), while Carol took the other children to the river. We enjoyed our hour together, and after buying the uniform went and had coffee. Throughout Mark's illness special times alone with the girls had to be sought out and savoured. I was very aware of the impact of Mark's illness and death on them and had looked for advice on how to help them.

A few months previously I had searched quite hard for any literature which would help us and had had very little success. A year later, some months after Mark's death, the appropriate books seemed to fly off the shelves at me! Where had they been the year before when I had needed them, these books on caring for a dying child, on the spirituality of children, and in particular on dying children and reactions to bereavement? Most had been published longer than a year. However, I have concluded that it was right that we didn't read them during Mark's illness. Some of the things they said about the way parents and siblings might react would have worried me if I had read them before Mark had died. I also feel that we 'did it our way', uninfluenced by the thoughts of others. Mark's faith and spirituality developed from within him, not due to prompting from us, even if that had been possible. If I had read the books I might have looked for things that were not there. Since Mark died, however, I have found these books and the study of bereavement in general very helpful and interesting.

However, in this dearth of literature two very helpful articles by Mother Frances Dominica of the childrens hospice in Oxford, Helen House, did come to light. One dealt with the spiritual aspects of death and the other, written for the British Medical Journal, dealt with practical aspects. I had many ideas about what I would want to do and not want to do if and when Mark died. Mother Frances helped me to see that what we feel to be instinctively right is indeed right for us and that other people should realize this. It helped remove a fear that I might be badgered into conventions I did not want.

We went to Carol's for a week and had a wonderful holiday despite cold weather. Mark seemed very well and crawled easily from room to room, his speech still fairly clear. He wasn't frustrated and thoroughly enjoyed his holiday. He and Louise kept a diary of all we did, visiting the railway museum at Bressingham, hanging over the bridge catching crabs at Walberswick, Jake's third birthday, a children's play in the village hall, a visit to the butterfly farm. One day Carol took all the children to the seaside, leaving Derek and me alone for the day. It was a miserable day. We found no joy in each other's company and I was quite worried. Many marriages break up under the strain of losing a child. But I am sure we were just miserable about Mark as we visited places we had last been to with him when he was well. Our marriage has in fact survived all the trauma quite intact.

Mark had put on a lot of weight and needed new clothes. While shopping for the clothes he treated himself to a personal stereo cassette player out of his holiday spending money.

Derek, Mark and I returned home at the end of the week, leaving the girls at Carol's for another week. Now each night after his story and prayer time I would leave Mark listening to a tape on his personal stereo. After a while a yell would prompt us to turn the tape over and some time later another would signal that the tape was finished and he was settling down to sleep!

Despite his growing collection of 'Jesus books' we had not been very successful in finding 'Jesus stories' on tape, but one he had was David Kossoff reading his story of the 'Three Donkeys'. Events in Jesus' life are recalled by three donkeys getting together in heaven to reminisce. One night Mark settled down to listen to the story at bedtime. The usual yell signalled half time but instead of settling down to sleep at the end he became agitated, saying 'It hasn't finished.' We showed him that the tape had finished but he was insistent and became more and more upset. So we listened to the end of the tape. It ended with the donkey describing the empty tomb. No risen Jesus. Mark was quite right: the story was not finished!

Mark woke up on our first morning at home with a cold and was plainly worse than he had been. Again his dependence on steroids made even a common cold a more serious affair and much more difficult to throw off. I had expected that he would get colds and chest infections which might accelerate his death, but I hadn't expected them in the middle of August! At bedtime that night during Mark's prayer time we prayed that Jesus would make his cold better. The next day he suddenly announced that it was. I realized the congestion was a lot easier during the day and

81

expected it to come on again at bedtime but he told me his cold was better. Jesus, 'the one who is always with him' (his words), had told him so. And he was right. That cold, which could have made his final weeks such a misery, was gone, never to return.

The phone rang about half-past four that afternoon and David, my brother-in-law, told me that Louise had broken her arm falling off a playground roundabout and was in hospital waiting for it to be set under general anaesthetic. A friend came round to look after Mark and within an hour I was on my way to Bury St Edmunds! Louise's need was greater than Mark's at that time. She is the most stoical of the three and if she said she wanted me she really did! We waited nearly all the evening for her arm to be set while she became more and more tired, hungry and frightened. But eventually it was all done, a night in yet another children's ward was over and we were all on our way home to Maidenhead. Louise very rapidly became quite proud of her arm once it stopped hurting and she loved being the centre of attention for a while.

The weather had turned very warm and the heat made Mark weak. We realized he was getting slowly worse. He crawled for the last time. His speech was more difficult to understand. His breathing was rapid and shallow and I wondered if he was going to get pneumonia again. Yet we still enjoyed some more outings and another short holiday with his godparents.

While Mark had been so well for so long it had become harder to accept that he was dying, for there was more to lose. As he started to get much worse again his death became easier to accept. But I realized that Derek had still not reached this acceptance. He still saw Mark's death as being months away. Even without my conviction that he would die in September I would not have expected him to last until the winter at the rate he was deteriorating. My worst fear was that he would suffer severe incapacitation for a prolonged time. This would have put a strain on us and been so unfair to Mark. I tried to explain to Derek that I thought that when the autumn came Mark might well fall prey to infections which would cause his death.

As his speech again deteriorated I found him almost impossible to understand at times, but he never gave up trying to say what he wanted. Sometimes I only wished he would. He just became more and more agitated, which made the speech even worse! Eventually I would realize what he was saying. Selfishly, I was more frustrated at my inability to understand than aware of his frustration at being unable to talk properly and particularly to interrupt. It was only after Mark had died that a friend lost her voice completely and for the first time I realized just what torment he must have suffered. While he was alive I was too involved to fully appreciate it.

As the last week of the holidays progressed Mark's deterioration seemed more rapid. I realized how much less he was sleeping. The pressure of the tumour was now keeping him awake rather than sending him to sleep. He began to lose his balance when kneeling on the floor and we had to surround him with cushions.

Through much of Mark's illness Derek came home for two mornings a week and sometimes this gave me the opportunity for a short break; otherwise I was with Mark twenty-four hours a day.

Over the next few weeks our family life became centred on our bedroom. We even sat in there and ate in order to be with Mark. When we were at home he was most comfortable on the bed, leaning on loads of pillows but always kneeling with his legs under him. This position prevented the spasms in his legs which were both uncomfortable and painful.

Being in the bedroom so much was made easier by our having a bungalow, and friends got used to letting themselves in at the front door.

Large parts of my day were spent sitting on our bed with Mark, cuddling him, watching television with him, and reading to him. He was now so wakeful that he frequently didn't fall asleep until I went to bed, and he was awake very early in the morning. Friends from the church began to call more and more frequently, developing a rota between them so that we were seldom alone. Peter began to visit nearly every day.

However it was not the end of our outings. We continued to put Mark in the car. As he became weaker he rested on a pillow with the seat belt fastened around him, and we were able to push him around town in the buggy.

He was by now so weak that he was frustrated much of the time. He still tried to talk and was almost incomprehensible. One night he was awake for a long time trying to tell or ask me something. I just could not understand. We both got upset; it was awful. I began to feel that his death would bring relief. He didn't talk again. For a couple of days his left arm was sufficiently strong for him to write a letter, either on paper or traced on the floor. From this we could guess what he wanted. When his right hand was no longer able to hold a pen, he had changed without comment to using his left hand for a short while until this too became too weak.

Later I would write out the alphabet and he would point to a letter. He was able to nod and shake his head in answer to our questions, but very soon the only communication we had was, as in hospital the year before, through his eyes. Even so, I could understand most of his needs. He was now finding it very hard to eat and even drink. Swallowing became almost impossible and even giving him his medicine was fraught with difficulty. I feared he would choke to death on it.

For a short while he was still able to suck through a straw, but soon the only way to give him a drink was almost to pour it into his mouth, a messy procedure. His breathing was becoming noisy and I suspected a build-up of fluid on his lungs, although we later found his lungs were clear. The congestion was in the throat and could have been alleviated with suction.

11

The Last Weeks

I dreaded the girls going back to school, as they were such a help and company for me. The day before the new term started Sue came to see us. Mark had made up his mind we would have a Chinese take away meal when Sue came and wouldn't be deterred, even though he found it almost impossible to eat. The meal was a nightmare. He wanted to eat, and I had to put food in his mouth. Then he was sick. I still found grains of rice in his mouth the next morning. From then on he ate nothing except jelly and more jelly, which we more or less poured down his throat. I could see no point in tube feeding him. Going without food didn't distress him and was a natural part of his dying. At times he scarcely drank enough but showed few signs of dehydration.

I was concerned about Elizabeth having to start at a new school under such difficult domestic circumstances but needn't have worried as she was given so much loving attention. She went off happily to her first day at school and settled in very quickly.

Mark and I continued to take Louise to school by car whenever we were able but Celia and another neighbour were on hand to help out whenever they were needed.

Mark's wakefulness and agitation was now such that I phoned the hospital. He was also having problems again passing urine.

The hospital suggested that I ask our GP for diazepam for him to help him sleep and just take the edge off his awareness. We decided to insert a catheter and to avoid taking Mark anywhere to have this done David, although no longer at the Radcliffe, came from Oxford to do it.

For three weeks before his death Mark was virtually unable to do anything. He seemed to linger unnecessarily long but with hindsight we could, as on so many other occasions, see the value of this. During this time Derek finally accepted that Mark would soon die, and Mark himself came to terms with his death.

When we had returned from holiday I was aware that Mark hadn't long to live and also that whilst we were away our nightly chats had ceased. I started to be a lot more explicit to Mark about his death, although we never actually used that term, always talking in terms of going to be with Jesus and the joy that would bring him. One of his favourite stories was 'Charlotte the Caterpillar'. Charlotte could never believe it when she was told that caterpillars hatch from butterfly eggs and that she would herself one day become a butterfly, until . . .

At that moment she felt something at her side. She looked round – eight or ten little green caterpillars were moving about and had already made quite a hole in the cabbage leaf! They had broken from the butterfly's eggs!

Charlotte was filled with astonishment – and then with joy. For since one wonder was true, perhaps the others were too.

The caterpillar talked for the rest of her life to her friends about the time when she would be a butterfly. But none of them believed her.

. . . when she was going into her chrysalis grave, she said, 'I shall be a butterfly some day.'

And when she was a butterfly and was going to die again, she said, 'I have known many wonders. I have faith – I can trust even now for what shall come next!'

Mark loved this story and told me it was about dying. I read it to him once again and was more frank than ever before about what was happening to him. This coincided with him being unable to speak any more and I was concerned that he was unable to ask any questions. Had he in fact been trying to when he attempted to talk that last time and gave up? Whatever the reason, there was a definite cooling off in his enjoyment of his 'Jesus stories'. Perhaps it was just a little too close for comfort. I continued to read one each night but sensed a lack of empathy between us. However he still enjoyed his prayer times and I was also able to use my prayers in a teaching way.

All of a sudden a fortnight later, just eight days before he died, I sensed that Mark was 'with me' again. I read the story of Easter from his children's Bible. At a good stopping point I suggested that we continue the next day. He wouldn't have that and once again he couldn't have enough of his stories about Jesus. I believe that during that two weeks Mark had done a lot of thinking and had at last accepted his death. He had done his grieving for his own life. That night was the only night in weeks that he went to sleep soon after seven and didn't wake until the morning. A natural, peaceful sleep.

All through these last weeks Mark's 'office' lived on a low trolley in our bedroom. Even when totally unable to do anything he would indicate that he wanted to play with it. I, groaning inwardly, would then support him on the floor and play a question-and-answer game (feeling that I sounded like a computer) in order to find out what he wanted moving and where!

In those last weeks with a constant stream of visitors our bedroom was such a happy, peaceful place, often filled with the sound of much laughter. Gill now came frequently and did the ironing rather than take it home with her. Other friends would sit and read Mark a story, while I stretched my legs and made coffee. One morning Peter arrived with a joke book and for some time kept Mark amused while Gill and I groaned at the awful jokes. Mark and Peter's particular favourite was: 'Where do you take a sick wasp? To the 'Waspital'!! Peter then had to copy out many of the jokes into one of Mark's files.

The girls were forced to be self-sufficient during those weeks. They had a school dinner, but frequently had to get their own tea. Once or twice Mark slept during the late afternoon and one of them would sit with him while I prepared a meal. They were very good with Mark and shared in reading stories and playing games, or just sat with him and watched television.

The weekends were probably the most difficult. On Saturday mornings we went to the church for coffee but the afternoons always dragged. It was the one time in the week when we didn't have visitors, everyone being busy with their families, but of course Derek was at work. On Sundays we took to going to McDonald's for lunch. It was the easiest thing to do. Preparing a meal at home was difficult and to go anywhere else meant a waiter coming to the table. In the anonymity of McDonald's it didn't matter that Mark wasn't eating.

The weeks without eating were taking their toll and Mark had lost a great deal of weight. However because of his previous steroidal bloatedness this just had the effect of returning him to the Mark we recognized. Without the steroids I dread to think what he would have looked like.

To the uninitiated Mark appeared semi-conscious, but although he was totally incapacitated his brain worked normally! He still knew exactly what he wanted to do and more especially what he didn't! As I have said before, we were not being cared for by people experienced in caring for terminally ill children and I had to remind even those in the medical profession that Mark was listening and taking in everything they said and that they could speak to him. I wouldn't have got away with taking him anywhere he didn't want to go or making him do anything he didn't want to do. His pleasures were simple. Choosing a poster together in the Christian bookshop, a helium-filled balloon, lots of cuddles, the feel of the warm water around him in the bath. Even so, he still directed me round the shops with a pointing finger and one day chose yet more pens for his office!

Throughout these weeks I felt so sustained and supported that I was effectively feeling very 'high'. I had endless energy, was efficiently organized and seemed to have endless resources to cope, although during this time I ate very little and lost nearly half a stone. I was certainly given the physical and mental strength to cope at the time. Now, I sometimes wonder how I did. Before, I wondered how I would cope, but we are given the strength when we need it, not before and not after. I was irritated by my mother and the health visitor trying to suggest to me that I didn't realize what was happening. I didn't need anyone to tell me how much it hurt to watch your child die! I didn't need telling how long it would take me to get over it afterwards! However, I was aware that when Mark died one of my initial emotions would be that of relief, for him and us. These last weeks seemed so long it hardly seemed fair on Mark. I no longer prayed for his healing of body but that he be released from his suffering.

I prepared the girls as best as I could, telling them that any day they might wake up or return from school to find that Mark had died. Louise was disturbed. 'No', she said, 'he'll be in hospital.' I explained that Mark would die at home. This obviously worried her. Further probing revealed that she had seen a man die, apparently from fright, in a detective story on television. He had died with mouth open wide and eyes popping out of his head and stayed like that! This was Louise's picture of death. I reassured her that he would just look as if he was asleep and she was much happier. Another example of the reality not being as bad as the fear and that it is best to involve children fully and explain everything. Their anxieties are often compounded by adults who think they are protecting them.

During the last week of Mark's life we watched him gradually lose interest in the things of this world. He scarcely watched television, wanted fewer stories, was content just to lie and do nothing. His cry was now no more than a whimper. His breathing and pulse rates were very high, as the tumour interfered with their control, and he was becoming very cyanosed, a blue tinge to his skin. One night his congestion was so bad it was only by changing his position that I prevented him from suffocating. Although I now prayed for his death, I couldn't have allowed him to suffocate.

Sunday came and with it Harvest Festival. I asked Mark if he wanted to come to church with me, intending to leave early in the service when he had had enough. We sat very near the front, Mark lying in my arms. As the service progressed I kept asking Mark if he was enjoying it and if he wanted to leave now. Each time he indicated that he wanted to stay. It was a wonderful service of thanksgiving. Towards the end of the service Peter asked the congregation to move round the church saying thank you to one another for anything they received. He immediately swept over to us, enveloped Mark in his arms and thanked him for being his friend. He was rewarded by Mark's acknowledgement. Unable to smile, Mark responded with his eyes, returning the love. But Peter was gone before I could thank him for all the love and support he had shown us. And where was

Gill when I wanted to thank her for all her love and practical help? I had to thank them both afterwards. The service finished with the hymn 'Now thank we all our God', a hymn we'd had both at our wedding and at Mark's baptism. I sat, cuddled Mark, and cried as if my heart would break. Many of the congregation cried with me. Would I ever sing that hymn again without tears?

Often during those last weeks of Mark's life I worried about how he would die. I feared that I might be chatting to friends and would look down to find he had died unnoticed. I seldom left him when he was awake, afraid to miss his last conscious moments. I still found it difficult to realize that he would die. I accepted that he was dying, but it was a new experience for me and I couldn't imagine it happening. However, when the time did come for Mark to die it was a beautiful experience with him being the centre of attention in a scene that could have been stage-managed!

12

'Free to Dance'

I woke up very early on Monday 28 September 1987 to find Mark with alarm in his eyes awake beside me. He was obviously distressed and I discovered he had a pain in his head. I rang the doctor, who suggested I give him all his drugs including paracetamol and the diazepam and ring her again before she went to the surgery if he didn't settle. I threw some clothes on and returned to Mark. I asked Derek to stay at home, realizing Mark had taken a turn for the worst and suspecting his death wasn't far away. I sat on the bed and cuddled him. He soon settled down and was obviously happier, relaxed and peaceful. A little later I looked down at him, noticed he looked different and realized his pupils were like pinpoints. He had slipped into a coma. The doctor rang and said that it would only be a shallow one or his pupils would dilate. I resolved to assume that he could hear us at all times. The girls went to school.

Gill arrived. She had been calling in nearly every day for the last week, and as the morning progressed our bedroom filled up with friends. Assuming Mark could hear we played his favourite tape of children's hymns. The doctor called. We were all quiet, watching every breath Mark took, realizing that very soon would come the last. A little later Peter came, held Mark's hand, and prayed with him and us. 'Jesus said, "Peace I leave with you, my peace I give to you;

. . . let not your heart be troubled, neither let it be afraid.'
The Lord is my shepherd; I shall not want . . .'

As Peter finished praying, Derek, almost overwhelmed,
left the room, followed quickly by Peter, who went to
comfort him. We put the tape back on. After a short while
Mark's breathing pattern changed, each breath becoming a
short gasp. I called Derek and Peter back. They came quickly
and climbed on to the bed to be close to Mark.

For a second the situation almost overwhelmed me. I
struggled to stay 'inside' it and succeeded. I had always
been able to cope because I was so involved. I was 'inside'.
If I stood back and looked in, it was horrific.

Time seemed to stand still. Mark lay in my arms, Peter
and Derek were sitting on the bed, the others all standing
or sitting around the bed. Peter was praying again. Mark's
breathing seemed to stop. I thought he had died when he
took two more breaths and turned his head to rest it on my
breast, his eyes fixed on my face. His favourite hymn, Lord
of the Dance, was playing. Mark, released from the cocoon
of his body, was free, completely healed, free to dance with
the Lord of the Dance.

I rested my hand gently on his chest. 'He's not breathing
any more.' 'No,' said Peter softly. We all cried.

Would Mark miss us as much as we would miss him? I
am confident that the joy of being with his heavenly Father
more than compensates for the absence of earthly parents
and am comforted by the thought that God's time is not our
time and it will seem no time at all to Mark until we are
reunited. Also, as friends sought to find appropriate words
during those first few hours, an oft repeated phrase was
'he's running around in heaven now'. Yes, imagine his joy
at being freed from that restricting body, free to dance, free
to run!

What other than joy could there be for a little boy for

whom Jesus had been so important. How he loved Jesus! How precious those 'Jesus books' were! His joy in sharing in the communion service, his delight in the story of the risen Lord leading to his hope of being united for ever with Jesus in heaven. How hard we had prayed that Mark be physically cured! This was not to be, but he became whole spiritually. In losing his life he has found the joy of eternal life in Jesus. He can no longer suffer. Not for Mark the temptation of drugs or alcohol, the pain of broken human relationships. He has found Jesus as a little child and can now never be lost to him.

We had so often likened death to metamorphosis, but it was months after Mark died that in the words of a poem I read I saw those last three weeks of his life as a cocoon, when trapped by his body the change was taking place inside as he accepted his death and made himself ready to meet Jesus.

One of the things I had dreaded about Mark's death was his being taken away. Since reading the papers by Mother Frances of Helen House I realized that if we wanted to we could choose to keep Mark at home until the funeral. I had planned in my mind many times in the days before he died what I would do. First I laid him in my mothers arms for a few minutes, then carried him into his bedroom and put him into his own bed.

A little later, with a friend's help, I washed and dressed Mark in a red jogging suit he had often worn during the summer. We spent time choosing which socks we would put on him, which seemed ridiculous and we laughed at ourselves. We pinned his cross to his cardigan. We had difficulty closing his eyes, he had slept with them open for so long. Eventually we left them a little open but that looked quite normal for Mark. His body still limp and warm, I was able to give him a last cuddle. Mark had no further need for his body, it was only an empty shell, but it still represented my child and I had very strong opinions about what I wanted to happen to it. I didn't want him handled by strangers or to be taken to a strange place. I wouldn't have wanted anyone else to lay him out. They might have combed his hair – how he would have hated that!

We planned that he would lie in his own bed for a couple of days and then be taken to the church until the funeral. For that first day we didn't even shut his bedroom door, so that there was no feeling of shutting him away.

There were telephone calls to make. So many people to let know. I was surprised to find that I was able to tell people that Mark had died. I had been expecting Mark's death for so long I was relieved it was over and had happened in such a lovely way. I didn't consciously feel shock but kept shaking and was quite unable to eat. Grief is very physical, felt in a knotted stomach, restricted throat, throbbing head, trembling limbs, almost everywhere but the heart! I wasn't dazed, though. We had started to grieve the previous New Year's Eve. I never experienced that feeling of being in a daze again. In many ways we felt we had already done a lot of our grieving in the months of preparation for Mark's death.

I phoned both schools and arranged to go and collect the girls. At each school we were given a room to be alone to tell them. We brought them home and took them to see Mark. Elizabeth was slightly reluctant but we felt it in her best interests to insist. However, she was not happy about him being at home. Louise was very natural. She wandered in and out to see Mark whenever she wanted to. We felt it was most important to include the girls in all the arrangements and give them adequate opportunity to grieve.

The next days brought a stream of visitors who hugged us, cried with us, and comforted us. Many were able to see

Mark and some experienced great peace as a result. For us his presence was a healing experience. Gradually as the days passed we wanted to go to him less and less. His features began to change slightly. He looked less and less like Mark, only the curly hair remained the same. When, two days later, they took him to lie in the church, in his coffin lined with his Thomas the Tank Engine duvet cover, I was able to let him go quite happily. It wasn't Mark any more. I was able to let his body go. I have heard grieving described as the gradual and very painful severing of every tie to the loved one who has died. In letting Mark's body go I had begun that process.

The first night I slept very little and with Elizabeth watched most of the all night television programmes! Louise chose to go to school the next morning but Elizabeth stayed at home. She went in the afternoon but found it difficult and stayed at home for the rest of the week. I was content to indulge her. There would be no question next week.

Peter called in frequently during the next few days. He was with us late in the evening on the Tuesday and prayed with us before leaving. He left me feeling very peaceful and I had no more problems sleeping.

The funeral was arranged for the Friday. We had long ago decided Mark would be buried and not cremated. Although I had always been an advocate of cremation, I found I couldn't have Mark cremated. We never know how we will react until we are in a particular situation.

We went to register Mark's death. I was not worried about going. I have registered deaths before and saw it just as a formality. Until the registrar asked for his date of birth. I had been there at his birth and his death! It seemed to knock me sideways. It was as if he had been signed on and now off. He had been and now he was gone and that was that!

The pain was almost unbearable. I thought I would never stop crying. I felt exhausted.

I discovered that week two types of tears. The type of grief I experienced after registering Mark's death was acutely painful. It seemed as if I would never feel better, the tears never stop. When they began to abate, as they always did, I would be left feeling utterly exhausted. Other tears, like those brought on by reading any of the dozens of letters and cards that were arriving with each post, were healing tears. They made me feel good, and when they were over I was better.

Nearly two hundred letters and cards were sent to comfort us, from friends, acquaintances, nurses from the hospital, customers, teachers, parents of Mark's friends, even people we didn't know. Opening a letter from the family of one of Mark's friends I wanted to tell him and gradually the awareness that I could no longer tell him things began to dawn. Letters from Christian friends echoed our faith and hope: 'Mark is with Jesus', 'Our sadness is for ourselves, not for him.' One of my fellow church stewards wrote words I have repeated so many times:

> So many of us can remember Mark as he was – a *real* boy dashing here and there, bright and alert. We're sure that now, unfettered by his sickness, he is free to grow and develop as he was created to do. Free now to dance with the Lord of the Dance.

All assured us of their prayerful support of which we were already feeling the benefit. Edward wrote a letter to Mark: 'I am sorry you are deid (his spelling), I love you.'

At Alwyn school the head took all the children who had been in Mark's class and one or two others who had known him into the spare classroom to share her sad news. Some already knew or had guessed. She then said to them, 'I'm going to remember Mark when he was happy. I remember when I read him a story and he laughed and laughed and laughed.' She related to me how one after another the children came out with their own memories of Mark, quite unprompted by the teachers. Each child had then drawn a picture of a happy memory of Mark (the motor bike featured prominently) and the teacher wrote a caption to each picture according to what the child told her. The pictures were bound into a book and sent to us as a wonderful memory of all the happy times Mark had at school and the lovely friends he made.

During the year of Mark's illness we had taken hundreds of photographs. An attempt to preserve the image of what we might lose. As soon as Mark died I wanted none of those photographs and sought out all I could find of him before he was ill. It was as if I wanted to forget that part of his life. His illness loomed so large I had almost forgotten what he was like before. I filled the house with pictures of Mark from babyhood until his fifth birthday. I wanted to show all those who would be coming to the house the Mark we had actually lost a year before.

On Wednesday morning Derek and I arrived home to find the kitchen full of friends preparing a chicken casserole and cleaning out the fridge. How I appreciated their help! They didn't ask what to do, they got on and did it.

When Mark was taken to the church that afternoon we followed and with Peter and his wife Celia celebrated communion.

During that week and for sometime after I was on a different plane. I felt as though I was being carried along on Jesus' shoulder. As the week went on and people came to see us I found that they were crying and I was comforting them! Once again we were so strong, upheld by so much prayer.

The experience of Mark's illness had increased my personal faith in Jesus. In his death I found a new boldness. I found myself relating first to Peter and then to others many of the experiences I had had during the year. My faith was no longer something private. It was to be talked about. I had to proclaim the strength God had given me to help me overcome all this tragedy and difficulty. For the first time I told of hearing the words 'twelve weeks' spoken to me in prayer when I had no idea how long Mark would live. He had indeed lived about this length of time.

Peter came to discuss the service, which was to be a joyful thanksgiving for Mark's life and I told him which hymns and readings I would like. I had already asked Gill to sing. We all wondered how we would cope. For Peter it would be a traumatic occasion. But, as he said, if we all stopped to cry it wouldn't matter. My prayers in those few days were very much for Peter and for Gill and the roles they would play on Friday.

13

Thanksgiving

Friday, the day of the funeral, dawned clear and bright. We had slept well and were ready to face the day. We had given careful thought to what we would wear. I was certainly not going to wear black. This was going to be a service of thanksgiving, not sadness. I chose the white jumper and skirt I had worn to church the previous Sunday.

We had flowers from the family only and asked for donations for the children's ward at the Radcliffe Infirmary. We filled the church with flowers and I put a single red rose on the communion table. When Mark was born he was welcomed, like all babies in our church, with a rose, and I wanted to mark his birth to a new life with Jesus in the same way.

Derek, the girls and I met Peter in the vestry. I didn't want to parade into church following Mark's coffin. As he was already in the church this was unnecessary, so when the time came for the service to begin we walked in with Peter from the front, having had a prayer with him first. I was praying so hard for him, for the strength for him to get through the service, I didn't think much about myself.

As we walked into the church I was thrilled to see it full of people. The wreaths had been laid along the kneeler around the communion rail, with the cross from us and the posy from the girls on top of the coffin.

A large teddy bear made entirely of flowers caught my

eye and for some reason brought me nearer to tears than I was at any other time that day. Many people visited Mark's grave just to see that teddy.

Peter, his voice full of emotion, announced the first hymn, Mark's favourite, 'Lord of the Dance'. Peter spoke of God's continual presence with us in all circumstances, how Mark was continuing in that presence and that we would meet again in Jesus. He thanked God for Mark's life and for all who had cared for him, acknowledging in that care the gift of the Holy Spirit, enabling the quality of care Mark enjoyed. He peppered his talks with anecdotes about Mark, referring to his developing spirituality, even raising a laugh when he said he thought Mark would have rather been given a McDonald's chip or a black jelly baby at communion instead of a piece of bread!

Gill sang the hymn we had had at Mark's baptism, 'God make my life a little light', and Peter read Mark's favourite Bible story of the risen Jesus appearing to Mary in the garden.

The words of Romans chapter 8, which Peter read from the Living Bible, was affirmation of my faith and of my trust in God that from the tragedy of this situation would come good and that nothing could happen to me that would ever separate me from God's love.

The last words of the final hymn were 'My Saviour has my treasure, And he will walk with me.' I know that truth in my life. But I couldn't help but see Mark as my 'treasure' and know that my Saviour does indeed have him!

As we walked down the aisle behind Mark's coffin I was elated and full of God's strength and peace, feeling I wanted to greet people I saw with a smile. As we left the church to the echoes of 'Praise him with alleluias, for Jesus is Lord!' I had such a feeling of triumph.

At the cemetery we followed Mark's coffin on a very old

hand cart to the grave side. The coffin was lowered, Peter said more prayers and Psalm 23, and the service was over.

We drove home. I wondered if people would think it strange that I didn't cry. I was not being deliberately strong, I had no desire to cry. I truly enjoyed the day and had an overwhelming sense of peace and triumph. We were asked if we were taking tranquillizers! We didn't need them. In any case, even if we had been tempted we would have resisted. Grief is a naturally healing process, and any artificial aid to numb the hurt only interferes with that process and, I believe, causes more problems later on.

At home friends had shared in providing a buffet lunch and we had a happy time. As the afternoon wore on exhaustion began to hit me and I longed for the moment when everyone would be gone and I could relax, for the first time not minding about being alone. As renewed grief hit me in the evening Derek tried to comfort me and asked me to pray, and for the first time, apart from the children's bedtime prayers, we prayed together as a family.

We visited Mark's grave over the weekend to see all the flowers again, but I felt no great draw to the cemetery, no feeling that Mark was there. I've visited the cemetery when I've felt like it, much less often as time has gone on. Sometimes it makes me sad, sometimes not. I was there at lunch time one day and discovered that the sound of the children playing in the playground at Alwyn school can be heard there!

I went to church on Sunday. Often it is weeks before a bereaved person feels able to return to church. I couldn't have stayed away. It was part of my strength and I found I was less emotional in services now Mark had died! Derek, never very regular at church, came with me and began to attend frequently, also realizing where his strength came from.

Mark's story was now complete, the rest is our story. The story of months and years of grieving and coming to terms with Mark's death. A time of growing nearer still to God, feeling his presence, knowing his presence in our suffering. I shouldn't imagine that we will ever totally get over losing our child but we have learned to live again, not to be fettered by the experience but to grow through it to greater emotional and spiritual maturity. Many months before Mark died Peter had assured me that I would 'survive'. Although at times the pain has been almost unbearable, I am convinced that I have not only survived but in Christ I have triumphed.

Grieving is not a pleasant process but it is a necessity, slow and painful, until memories bring happiness and not pain. The depth of pain experienced is a testament to our love. If complete healing meant an attitude as if Mark had never existed I wouldn't want it. He is part of my life, one of my children. To completely exclude him would not be healing, it would be burying the hurt. The loss of your child must be different from all other bereavement because it is outside the normal course of events. You don't expect to outlive your child. You gave life to that child and part of you really has died, your arms empty in a way that cannot be compared with anything else. Our faith and confidence is that Mark is with Jesus and for that we are happy, but it didn't stop us missing his cuddles, his fun, his giggle, and his mischief!

We felt very much in those early days that when someone dies slowly as Mark had done, the grieving begins before the death. However, the intensity of caring can bring you closer rather than help with the parting. The Mark we had known had gone the previous summer. Not to say that the time when he was ill wasn't a very special time for him and us, a time of development for him, and for us a year of savouring each event knowing it to be the last with Mark.

Thanksgiving

The weekend over, Derek went back to work, the girls to school. It was Monday morning, exactly a year since that first Monday morning home from hospital. The first day of the rest of my life. For the first time in twelve years I had the day completely to myself, the children at school. I felt suddenly as if I had lost three and a half years of my life. My youngest child was now nearly ten instead of six. Only two more years with a child at junior school instead of the expected five. But my life has moved in new directions and that is no longer a source of sadness.

That Monday morning, alone in the peace of the house, I turned to my Bible and opened it. A verse from Isaiah stared out at me: 'He will take care of his flock like a shepherd; he will gather the lambs together and carry them in his arms; he will gently lead their mothers.'

I was asked whether as a Christian I felt I ought to show strength as a witness to my faith and to support my belief that Mark was now with Jesus, which should be a cause for celebration and not sadness, or whether the strength I was so obviously showing was, for want of a better word, genuine. My answer to this is that there was nothing phoney. The strength was in my heart and not only my head. Part of it resulted from that familiar feeling of being upheld in prayer. Those prayers were being answered in a very special way and I had the confidence that when the bad times came as they surely must I would slip gently from being carried along on Jesus' shoulder into the warm embrace of his arms. There is nothing wrong in a Christian grieving. Jesus wept for Lazarus. He agonized in the Garden of Gethsemane. Life in Christ was never meant to be a bed of roses, just the sure knowledge that I can take all my pain and grief and lay it at the foot of the cross and that his love will sustain me through every trial. Jesus suffered whilst on earth, he even wished that suffering to be taken away, but he still faced the cross, and his friends and family suffered too in his death so that we could know the depth of God's love for us. I know that as each new pain of grief came our way Jesus was there suffering with and for us. We don't grieve for Mark. Strangely, I have never felt a sense of waste as so often happens when a young life is lost. Mark lived a very full if short life which now continues in heaven. No, our grief is for ourselves. We do miss him and look forward to the day when we will meet in the presence of our Saviour. But my hope in heaven is not hope of reunion with Mark. My great joy will be to live in the eternal presence of God; to have Mark at my side will be a bonus.

We seemed to slip into a new existence so easily that for a while it almost seemed as if Mark had never existed. It frightened me a little. I knew enough about grieving to know that it should not be suppressed. Bottling up of emotions can result years later in either physical or mental illness. I was afraid I was just burying it. Peter reassured me when I told him that I wasn't feeling anything. 'Oh, it will come', he said. I was still numb.

Many people, not least C. S. Lewis, have described the 'laziness of grief', the lack of energy or incentive to do anything not absolutely necessary. This was not my experience. At all times of crisis, including the time of Mark's death, the adrenalin flowed and with it came a surge of energy and activity which helped me keep on top of everything. I was able to take up new activities and commitments and resume ones I had been forced to put aside. I became a parent governor of Louise's school, began to run the church bookstall, organized the making of banners for the church hall as well as carrying out the duties which were mine as a church steward. This was a reaction to the restrictions on me when I was caring for Mark. In the midst of grief I was enjoying a new freedom.

However, grieving is an exhausting process and at times if I was tempted to do too much I got over-tired, and I was less able to cope emotionally. During those first weeks I mostly did exactly as I wanted. I spent a lot of time with friends, enjoying countless outings for coffee or lunch and the therapy of talking to them. In many ways it was like a long holiday. Initially I found that I didn't want to be at home very much, but, having gone out, I took a while to realize that I didn't have to rush back!

But I made sure this activity wasn't an escape, giving myself plenty of time to be still and to think as well. In that new freedom I found more time to be alone with God, to pray, read and study the Bible and just to be still and enjoy his presence. I deliberately made no major decisions, promising myself at least a year to drift before resuming any kind of career or vocation. I would wait until I knew what God wanted me to do with the rest of my life.

Both before and since Mark's death I had been urged by many people to write my experience down. Soon after Mark died I wrote an article which was published in *Magnet*, a Methodist women's magazine. I was beginning to testify publicly to the way in which God had brought me through this experience. Since then other occasions have arisen for me to give my testimony. The recording of our experiences, as well as enabling something positive to come from Mark's death, has been a therapy and healing, helping me to sort out my thoughts, encouraging the whole family to talk about Mark as we remembered him together, particularly the time before he was ill. It has provided us with a crystallization of memory and experience which we shall always have.

I had drifted through the first month without Mark. I was vaguely aware that I must get down to sorting out his things. There was no urgency but I felt that the longer I left it the harder it would be. We already knew what we would do with Mark's room. What else could we do but turn it into an office? After all, the notice was already on the door, and our present study was very small.

We finally started one Sunday afternoon, and by Tuesday morning most of Mark's things were sorted. There remained one box of toys to deal with. The box of cars, transformers, 'He-man' characters, etc. that he played with most. Gill was there to help me. Everything I picked up held a memory. I couldn't go on and had to put most of them away for another time. That afternoon we went to our Bible study group and during our prayer time my grief finally broke through the numbness. For days my heart ached, I longed for Mark, I could hardly bear to look at his photograph, tears flowed easily and readily.

The acuteness of grief faded over the next few days, to come and go as the weeks and months passed. Yet often in the midst of the worst agony I would be most deeply aware of the presence of Jesus bringing me peace.

People are frequently embarrassed in the presence of a bereaved person. They don't know what to say. We have all heard stories of people crossing the road to avoid speaking. I learned to handle this by making the approach myself. I don't think anyone avoided me. I'm afraid I didn't let them! However, people told me that I made it easy for them because I talked to them and enabled them to feel relaxed with me. It was all part of my determination to be positive and active rather than negative and passive.

14

Christmas Without Mark

The first year of any bereavement brings with it three major events which are likely to cause a renewal or new intensity of grief: Christmas, the birthday, and the anniversary of the death. I think that in mourning the death of a child the first two have an extra poignancy. For us Christmas was the first event to come rushing over the horizon. I wished it could have been cancelled.

I felt deeply involved in the religious festival but would have gladly forgotten all the secular trimmings. While the commercialism annoyed me, the 'baby in the manger' drew me to new experiences of worship. In my irritation with the secular I was drawn deeper into the true meaning of Christmas.

However, I still had daughters who, despite their own grief at the loss of their brother, couldn't fail to be excited as Christmas approached and if for no other than for their sake we had to have a good Christmas.

The problem of how to spend Christmas day was solved for us. Our church offered to host the Christmas lunch organised by the Christian Council in Maidenhead each year for the lonely. This year I would be preparing Christmas dinner for 120 instead of one less! In helping others we would be helping ourselves.

As in all aspects of grief, ignoring it or burying it doesn't make it go away, it only makes things worse, and we needed to acknowledge our grief to ourselves and admit what a gap there was in our family that Christmas. The children have always lit a candle before going to bed on Christmas eve, so we lit one for Mark as well. We sent a gift to the National Children's home as his Christmas present. Writing Christmas cards was particularly difficult with Mark constantly in my thoughts as I remembered to leave his name off. However, close friends may or may not have noticed the one kiss I added after our names. It all helped us to get through our first Christmas without Mark.

The girls decorated the house and we put up the tree. I found all this difficult but was able to look forward to Christmas day. Two years before, Mark's last Christmas before he became ill, the church had hosted the Christian Council meal and as a family we had gone to help with the tea. We had all had a wonderful time and it was a happy memory of our last 'normal' Christmas, so I knew that we would enjoy the day.

We did indeed have a wonderful time. Early in the day I felt numb again, a return to feeling nothing at all. The afternoon was lots of hard work but great fun. Linda and her family were also helping, so the girls were able to spend time with their friends, and the four of them together performed some sketches during the entertainment in the afternoon.

Later that evening as we relaxed, exhausted, at home Elizabeth exclaimed without thinking, 'That was the best Christmas ever!' Initially I was hurt but it proved I had achieved my aim to give the girls a good Christmas. Realizing what she had said, she was sorry.

When Mark died Derek and I felt we owed it to ourselves and to the girls to have a good holiday. The next summer seemed much too far off, so we planned a winter sun holiday in the Canaries straight after Christmas.

The packing done on Sunday in readiness for leaving on Monday, I suddenly felt full of grief again. I didn't want to go so far away! In church that night we read the story of Jesus being presented in the temple as a baby and Simeon's prophecy to Mary that '. . . sorrow, like a sharp sword, will break your own heart'. I knew all about what that felt like! I felt a deeper insight into the experience of Jesus' mother. I recently came across a short contribution I wrote for a Mothering Sunday service many years ago in which I had spoken of Mary's feelings as she watched her son die. What I had written from imagination I could now confirm and expand from experience.

The next day the excitement of going on holiday soon cut through the grief. But returning home was strange. Somewhere deep inside myself I had seen the passing of Christmas and our holiday as a new beginning. As though my unwritten period of mourning should now be over and when we got home everything would be all right again. This was obviously not so. Or perhaps I felt that other people would think that, and that my time of being indulged and fussed over was past. However, a new year and sun tan didn't make any difference to grief. Grief is no respecter of dates. I went briefly through a phase of guilt. Had I done everything for Mark that I could? Had I told him how special he was? Had I told him how much I loved him? Why hadn't I been more sympathetic towards him, understood his frustration more? All this is a natural part of grieving and I believe it is apt to come as the memory dims a little, as the bad times fade and only the good are retained. I poured it all out to Gill. Yes, I did tell him how special he was and how I loved him, she had heard me. And didn't I remember just how difficult he could be sometimes in those last few weeks? Gill said she would go home exhausted after a morning with us, aware that I had the rest of the day and the next and the next to cope with! Yes, I had done all I could. She helped tremendously and I soon stopped being bothered by this guilt. How important to share the problems as they arise and before they become insurmountable!

Early in January I visited the Radcliffe Infirmary with a cheque for nearly £1300. The memorial fund had risen over the weeks without any particular effort by us. The money was used to buy physiotherapy equipment for the children's ward and to contribute jointly with another ward to the making of a garden to provide a play area outside for the children. It helped to keep in touch with the hospital and for the first year or so we visited from time to time. I had been invited to the Christmas party and had enjoyed seeing lots of old friends. I was thrilled to see that Sarah, who had had radiotherapy at the same time as Mark, was fit and well, and found it very comfortable to talk to another mother whose child had died. We were relaxed in each other's company, not afraid of making the other feel awkward by talking of our son's death because of our shared experience.

I was beginning to realize that another way to turn my experience to good would be in support to the bereaved, perhaps even counselling, and as the months passed I began to become more interested in the subject of bereavement and to read widely about it, particularly in relation to bereaved children.

I have been conscious of the effects of Mark's illness and death on the children around him, particularly his sisters. They too were bereaved and had a lot of adjustment to make. In any bereavement sympathy often seems to centre on the adults and grieving children can be thought to be over their loss when they still hurt deeply inside but are unable to express it.

Although we involved the girls closely in Mark's care, their different relationships with him produced different reactions to his illness. Elizabeth and Mark were always close. Being nearly six when he was born, she had enjoyed caring for him as a baby, and as he grew up she often played with and helped look after him. This relationship continued and deepened in his illness. Louise, however, being the middle child, had a love-hate relationship with Elizabeth and Mark and squabbled with both. His illness put on her a pressure to change her relationship with him and made it more difficult for her to cope.

After Mark died Elizabeth appeared to me to grieve normally with frequent tears and she often talked about him. Then, suddenly one day about five months later, she realized that he wasn't coming back and was very upset for an hour or so. As time went on she felt guilty if she forgot him, because she didn't want to. We constantly assured her that all her feelings were perfectly normal.

Louise never seemed to cry and she worried me. She appeared to be frightened by tears, often encouraging me not to cry. About the time of Mark's birthday that first year she was sent in one lunch time at school for accidentally knocking over a little boy. The headmaster told me that her distress was out of all proportion to the incident. I probed later at home, and she eventually revealed to me in a letter that she had been crying about Mark. Writing it down helped her to admit it to herself. I was able to assure her that tears are OK and can make us feel better, and after that she was much happier. Louise missed Mark as a playmate, having at the same time lost a playmate in Elizabeth, who matured very rapidly while Mark was ill. At one point during Mark's illness Louise refused to go to Sunday School. We didn't force the issue and she came back of her own accord. A few months after Mark's death she herself took holy communion, and soon after both girls made a commitment to Jesus.

I have made sure that I haven't repeated the mistakes made by my grandmother, who had lost a six-year-old daughter. My mother grew up under the shadow of a little 'angel' who must surely have never done any wrong, and she was often told that her mother would have rather *she* had died. We have made quite sure that we remember Mark the little horror as well as all the good times! Also I try never to challenge the girls with 'Mark would or wouldn't have done that!'

Mark was always close to his cousins Katie and Jake. How would they react to his illness and death? Jake, two when Mark became ill, was too young to really understand or remember Mark before he was ill, although he still talks about him. Katie seemed frightened of Mark when he was first recovering but gradually accepted him as he was, although their previous relationship was not reestablished. She also had little memory of Mark as he had been, and after his death she said that thoughts of Mark made her want to cry. Unlike her brother, she has never wanted to visit Mark's grave. Again, Carol has assured her that this is all right.

Edward continues to remember Mark and for a while after his death talked about him every day. He wondered if God would smack Mark if he was naughty and if he had toys in heaven to play with. He has not been to the cemetery and has coped reasonably well with the idea of Mark happy in heaven. On one occasion when he had been told off he even suggested that he might quite like to join him!

One of Mark's little girl friends, Becky, who also has curly hair, has wondered if Mark's hair is still curly!

My whole attitude to Mark's death and the very roots of my faith were shaken suddenly one day when I read the words, not in the Bible but in Bible-reading notes, that, whatever happens, God is in control! I was shattered. In that case did God deliberately plan for Mark to become ill and die, or given that Mark was ill did he withhold healing? How could I love God if he took Mark away from me?

Distressed, I sought Peter's help. He helped me see it all in its larger perspective, that all that is uniquely Mark is now risen in Jesus. He stressed his belief that God in his great love for us could never will our suffering, but is with us in it, strengthening and enabling us. I could admit to the good that had come out of Mark's death in our own lives and in many around us. We had all learned and grown spiritually through our shared tragedy. Everything that Peter said I knew with my head. What I couldn't do was feel it in my heart.

Over the next few days I calmed down. The problem didn't seem so acute for most of the day, and I distracted myself that weekend by decorating the lounge. But whenever I came close to God I felt the barrier I had erected.

Five difficult days later I had a phone call asking me to talk about healing at a housegroup attached to Windsor Methodist church. The previous week Christopher Johnson had visited them and they were asking me to talk about our experiences with Mark and when the healing is not of the body. I was very hesitant because of the state I was in, knowing I could have done it a week before and would doubtless be able to do so in the future, but that now seemed quite the wrong time. I knew that the person asking me had prayed about whether he should ask me or not and was still unsure if it was the right thing for me. We agreed that I would pray about it and give him an answer in a few days.

I had no opportunity for prayer until I went to bed that night. I put the whole situation before God and immediately felt that I should get up again and write down all my thoughts about healing in relation to Mark, and tell the story of our visits to Christopher Johnson and all the subsequent events of Mark's illness. If I went to the meeting I would have all my notes ready, if I didn't I could send what I had written for someone to read.

I wrote until four o'clock in the morning and ended with some of the doubts and questions that I had.

'There are times when I am tempted to ask "Why?" about it all,' I wrote. 'Strangely not 'Why us?'', but "Why did this happen?" Could God have prevented Mark from dying? Is he working out some greater plan through Mark's death? I have no doubt that there is growth through suffering. I don't know the answers and am troubled by the questions, but I won't let them defeat me. I know the answers are probably beyond our human understanding and I have only to trust in God and in due time all will be revealed.'

I went to bed, had two hours sleep, and woke up feeling on top of the world. All my doubts had gone, healed by my airing of them: I had written them away. I went to the housegroup the following week and spoke for a long time without a trace of a tear! I was overwhelmed at the way God had healed me and used the story of the previous few days to start my talk.

I experienced a further confirmation of this healing a few weeks later. I went to a Quiet Day, a day's guided retreat in the peace and quiet of a convent but organized by the Methodist church. What a treat such a day is in the midst of our busy lives! A chance to forget the outside world and be still with God. During a period of silence I turned to one of the suggested Bible passages, knowing it to be one that brings me great comfort. How often had I read the words of Romans 8, but suddenly a phrase leapt out of the page at me and I saw with new eyes the words 'He who did not spare his own son . . .', God's only son given up freely for me. Yes, God actually *gave* his son: what was my loss of a son compared to that? For the first time I entered into the enormity of God's gift of his son, into the grief and suffering brought through that gift. All for the love of us. How often we know something for years and then some new insight helps us to realize it afresh. I had new insights into the heart of God that he could suffer such pain for me.

I no longer have doubts. I am sure that Mark's death was not part of some divine plan. God does not will or cause our suffering, but through and out of it he can and does bring good. There have been such blessings given to us through our whole experience. I have grown so much in my own spiritual experience that I am overwhelmed with thanks to God for Mark, for his life, for what I have learned and become through his death and for the tremendous privilege of being the mother of such a special child.

15

New Beginning

Grief is the process of healing that we go through following a loss of any kind. When that loss is the death of a loved one grief can be very long and painful. The pain and the heartache is actually physical at times and is a testament to our depth of love. Grieving cannot be hurried any more than can physical healing. Removing a scab too soon only opens up the wound again.

Only by airing every aspect of grief can we open it up for healing. Difficult situations need to be faced, the first time will always be the worst. Burying feelings and avoiding painful situations doesn't make them go away, they will only smoulder to surface in another time and place. Running away from a situation only puts it off for another day. A life governed by grief is not free. As more and more hurts are buried there is less and less freedom, for we become restricted to activities that don't cause pain.

About six months after Mark died I was offered the laying on of hands to heal me instantly from my grief! I declined and spent about half-an-hour talking my way out of the situation. Not that I was shy of the laying on of hands, but grief is a healing process, and how can you heal healing? My grief was important to me. Up to then I had an almost maudlin enjoyment of it. I read the words a widow wrote to her dead husband: 'If in my grief I can keep you close, I never want to feel better.' I could identify with that. I had a nostalgia for the time just after Mark's death when everyone was making a fuss of us and Mark still seemed close. I hated the passage of time as his death became first weeks and then months in the past.

However, at the time I was part of an event called Easter People, a holiday convention of worship, Bible study, and other activities organized by the Methodist church, and I was having a wonderful time. I actually wasn't grieving at all and it was a tremendous turning point in my grief. I felt great. We were staying near Rye and, walking through the streets, I was able to remember our weekend there soon after Mark had died and I realized that I was already building up a bank of happy memories without Mark. My grief was progressing normally. I would agree that outside help such as laying on of hands could be necessary if there is excessive guilt, bitterness, or prolonged grief, but these were not my experiences.

After the 'mountain top' experience of Easter People I slowly came down to earth in the first few days at home. After a week or so I felt the first few niggles of grief return. Now, having felt so free of grief, I didn't want it any more, resented it, and tried to bury it. Soon I was beginning to feel quite depressed and only felt better when I admitted to myself that I was grieving and let my grief out. I have often wondered how much more I might have resisted that grief had I received laying on of hands and what damage that might have caused.

As my grief renewed it became a form of regret. A very mild word for such an experience, but I was regretting the things we could no longer do with Mark, his presence in family activities, and his absence from any forward planning. They say that when you mourn a child you mourn for the lost expectations you have for that child. Perhaps this is so. It was never my obvious experience unless this feeling of regret encompassed it. However, it only lasted a short time.

As the months passed, more and more situations cropped up which needed to be faced and opened for healing. I would often dread annual events in both school and church but, having gone to them would find that, having faced them, I could enjoy myself. As a parent governor I was asked to attend the meeting for the parents and children who would be starting in the new term. Mark should have been one of those children and all his friends would be there. However, I decided I had to go. I had to face the fact that for the next year Louise would still be at Courthouse school, I would still be a governor, and Mark should have been in the first year. I prayed for the strength to cope, friends prayed for me, and once again the event was a complete success. The only emotion I felt all evening was that which I always feel when witnessing anybody at a point of change and growth in their life!

Mark's birthday was a slightly bigger problem. From the time when Mark died I couldn't bear to even think about his birthday. It was then so far off that the thoughts could be buried, but as the time approached it had to be faced, brought out into the open, acknowledged, and healed. I felt the tension begin to build in me as much as three or four weeks before. One or two friends asked how I planned to spend the day. I just didn't know. I wanted to be free to do just what I felt to be right at the time. I couldn't let the day pass unnoticed, after all it is an anniversary of a happy day in my life. The day I had a baby!

The weekend before it was, as always, the Church Anniversary, and all the talk of birthdays and anniversaries was almost too much to take, particularly everyone singing 'Happy Birthday' to the church!

Two days before Mark's birthday I sat in the garden

reading my Bible and enjoying a quiet time. My allotted reading for the day came from I Peter and included the words:

> Praise be to the God and Father of our Lord Jesus Christ. In his great mercy he has given us new birth into a living hope through the resurrection of Jesus Christ from the dead, and into an inheritance that can never perish, spoil or fade . . . In this you greatly rejoice, though now for a little while you may have had to suffer grief in all kinds of trials.

As I sat in the warmth of the sun aware that God understood the hurt that I felt I was overwhelmed by a wonderful sense of peace, which then carried me through the next few days. I recognized that feeling. Once again, aware of our particular need, friends were praying for us. I felt soaked in prayer.

From then on I looked forward to Mark's birthday with a sense of excitement and anticipation. It was still a special day and it felt special when it came. Not even particularly sad. I took flowers from the garden to the cemetery in the morning, for some reason wanting to be there at the time of day he was born, and found it very peaceful there.

We received flowers, cards, phone calls and visits. It was wonderful to be remembered in this way. Sometimes people don't like to remark on a birthday or anniversary of a death. But those who are grieving haven't forgotten, and you won't be reminding them or renewing their grief. Rather you will be showing you care, that you remember and that all helps in the healing. We even went out to dinner in the evening with Sue, who had come to spend the day with me. During the months before I would never have dreamed I would enjoy the day so much!

During Mark's illness we had talked about the possibility of having another baby, although before he was ill we were quite sure we had completed our family. Since my illness I had begun to get used to the idea that I might be unable to have any more children and I was reluctant to go down that road of raised and dashed hopes. I'd been there before! My sister's announcement about eight months after Mark died that she was expecting another aroused uncomfortable feelings in me, but I didn't really want a baby. My life had moved on from nappies and toddlers. If I wanted anything it would be a six-year-old, and not just anyone at that!

A couple of months later I was called for the laparoscopy operation I had been due to have just after Mark died. The letter calling me to hospital in two days time threw me into a whirl of preparation. Our business had expanded during the year and I helped out a lot, so work, children, and other commitments had to be organized. It was only a very minor operation but for some reason it worried me. I prayed and others prayed with me and soon I was off to hospital relaxing in the peace that only God can give. In hospital I had to explain to the nurse taking my details that Mark had died, because she had my old notes listing three children. Rather thoughtlessly she just crossed his name off. That hurt! However, the lady in the next bed had overheard and later told me that she admired me and wondered where I got my strength from. My prayer that I might have the opportunity to witness to God in that place had been answered!

During the operation the next day they decided that any further pregnancy would bring with it a high risk of another ectopic, and so they sterilized me.

A few days later the reality of this hit and I was very depressed. I had lost a lot in the last year. However, with the passing of time two things have happened. Any jealousy of my sister left me and I was able to welcome the birth of first a new nephew and then more recently another niece. The other thing is that I am now perfectly happy with the thought of having no more children. A couple of months after the sterilization I dreamt that I was pregnant and was horrified! Sometimes it takes a dream to face the reality of the situation. I realized the desire for another baby was a surface emotion brought on by the loss of Mark. We could never have replaced him. I needed to remember how I felt before he was ill, ready to branch out and do other things. Now I have moved on in so many ways that there is no gap in my life the size of a little boy of whatever age Mark would have been as the years go by. The Lord has other work for me to do.

The months of grieving passed by. At no time had I felt overburdened by my grief. It had never held me back or dominated my life. I continued to live and grow and be positive. This attitude was interspersed with patches of grief that became further apart and shorter in duration. I had been sustained throughout by my faith, through worship, my Bible study group, communion, and my private times where I could be quiet and alone with God. He has brought me through this experience and into a deeper relationship with him.

As time passed I was confronted by different attitudes in other people. Some after a few months seemed to expect me to have forgotten all about it, others seemed to want to label me forever a bereaved parent. As part of my experience my bereavement is part of the person I am, but I encountered an attitude that wanted to attribute every whim of my personality to my bereavement! Of course the truth lies somewhere between the two.

For a time I felt a great urgency to support the bereaved. Now I realize that this was partly my need to be with others in the same situation. Also I briefly held the attitude that if I could cope then so could everyone else and felt an irritation with those with lesser problems, but this too was just a phase of my own grief and soon I was led to a deeper sensitivity and compassion towards all suffering in others. We are all broken in some way and in our mutual brokenness we can minister to one another. I have had an experience which I can use to the benefit of others. I can face the dying without fear, the bereaved with empathy. We read in Paul's second letter to the people of Corinth 'the Father of compassion and the God of all comfort, who comforts us in all our troubles, so that we can comfort those in any trouble with the comfort we ourselves have received from God'. I can use this experience to help others who suffer in the same way. I don't pretend to know what others are feeling in their pain, but because I too have suffered I feel I can come alongside them. I think there was a time when I thought that through the renewing, healing power of God I would eventually be completely healed. Now I believe that however much God renews and restores me he does not undo or take away my experience. It remains as much a part of me as the marks of the nails on the hands of the risen Jesus, and just as he remains the crucified yet risen Lord so I am the person I am because of rather than in spite of my experiences. As time has gone on I have felt called by God to care for others in a much wider sense than the bereavement counselling I envisaged during that first year.

Another aspect of this has been a deepening sense of the hurt in the heart of God as he contemplates the suffering in his world, and this has led me to greater social concern and action. I have developed a strong awareness that each is God's child and loved by him, yet so many are denied fullness of life through oppression or deprivation. The death of a child, such a rare event in this country, is being needlessly repeated time and again in all parts of our world.

Once again September was drawing near. I suddenly realized that I would re-live the events of the previous year.

This didn't worry me. It would open up each memory for healing. I was actually unconcerned about the anniversary of Mark's death and in such a state of unpreparedness that it hit me like a sledgehammer. I didn't have to remember that it was September. Everything screamed it at me. The day length, having to put the lights on in the morning, the weather, the smells of autumn, the girls going back to school. The smell of the church for Harvest Festival brought another flood of memories, and finishing the evening service with 'Now thank we all our God' was the last straw. Celia Hudson, comforting me, said 'It doesn't get any better does it?' But it did. In a way, as the bouts of grief got further apart, they hit with renewed ferocity through their very unexpectedness. I felt an inexplicable urge to try and recreate the previous year. I would have liked to go to McDonald's for Sunday lunch, but we didn't. I wore the same clothes. Gill was affected in the same way, feeling she wanted to sing 'God make my life a little light' as a solo in church on the anniversary of Mark's funeral, which was a Sunday. This she did as it fitted well into the planned service.

Mark's headstone was erected on the anniversary of his death. I had ordered it on his birthday, the most expensive birthday present he ever had! We chose a plain, grey granite cross (I am sure he would have chosen a cross) and had a tablet inscribed:

Mark Geoffrey Austin
Died 28th September 1987
Aged 6 years
Free to dance with the Lord of the Dance

Once again as on Mark's birthday people showed that they remembered and shared our sadness, and soon the time was past and the sadness eased again. I was helped by a renewed experience of the Holy Spirit guiding my life and urging me into new ways of service, giving me that joy and peace welling up from within which can only come from God.

In my early teens I had felt called by God into some kind of full-time Christian service. As I grew up I had turned away from this, and now in the experience of Mark's illness and death I realized that because that sense of call had never left me I had erected a barrier between me and God, afraid to get too close to him for fear of what he might ask me to do, praying but being careful not to listen! Mark's illness had broken that barrier down, I had reached out to God, discovered in a new way that he loves me and now knew that whatever he wanted me to do with my life would be what I wanted to do, my only desire to love and serve him. At first I thought that my response to a call to be a Methodist Local Preacher was the realization of God's will for me but he has since led me into work as Lay Pastoral Assistant in the church.

I have talked a lot about my experience of Mark's death and the effect it has had on me. It is not so easy to describe the feelings of another, but Derek's life has been profoundly changed too. Always sympathetic to my activities within the church, he had never been a regular churchgoer. Since Mark's death he has found comfort in his developing Christian faith; he began to worship every Sunday, and has become involved in the life of our church. Just over a year after Mark's death he made a commitment to Christ and was confirmed. He can acknowledge that this is a direct result of Mark's death and he can sing with conviction, 'Jesus you are changing me' – as indeed he is!

I remember Derek's cry, so long ago during the night before we took Mark for that first brain scan, that he couldn't stand weakness. Months later he was prepared to accept

Mark in the weak state that he was rather than not have him at all. And now through the loss of Mark he has found a newness of life in his Christian faith.

Yes, our lives have changed, never to be the same again, but the change is not all for the worse. Of course I miss Mark and sometimes long to hold him. I doubt that will ever go. But my life has moved on in so many ways that there is no longer a gap. In company with every bereaved person I have made a choice between letting this tragedy end my life and making it a new beginning. Through the loss of Mark and the experience of his illness I have gained that most precious gift available to all, a life lived so much more closely with Jesus, filled with his Holy Spirit. I can surely say with St Paul that 'We know that in all things God works for good with those who love him, those whom he has called according to his purpose.'